CAKE DECORATING
STEP-BY-STEP

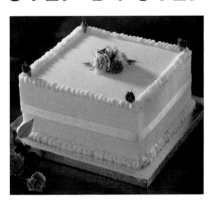

CAKE DECORATING
STEP-BY-STEP

Sensational cakes for any occasion made easy – from how to bake fantastic bases
to creating fabulous finishes with all types of icings, frostings and coverings

300 simple-to-follow colour photographs to help you achieve perfect results every time

Angela Nilsen and Sarah Maxwell

HERMES
HOUSE

This edition is published by Hermes House, an imprint of Anness Publishing Ltd, Hermes House, 88–89 Blackfriars Road, London SE1 8HA; tel. 020 7401 2077; fax 020 7633 9499 www.hermeshouse.com; www.annesspublishing.com

If you like the images in this book and would like to investigate using them for publishing, promotions or advertising, please visit our website www.practicalpictures.com for more information.

Publisher: Joanna Lorenz
Senior Managing Editor: Conor Kilgallon
Editors: Judith Simons, Clare Nicholson and Elizabeth Woodland
Photographer: Tim Hill
Home Economists: Sarah Maxwell and Angela Nilsen
Assistant Home Economist: Teresa Goldfinch
Stylist: Sarah Maxwell
Assistant Stylist: Timna Rose
Design: Axis Design
Cover Design: Nigel Partridge
Production Controller: Lee Sargent

ETHICAL TRADING POLICY

Because of our ongoing ecological investment programme, you, as our customer, can have the pleasure and reassurance of knowing that a tree is being cultivated on your behalf to naturally replace the materials used to make the book you are holding. For further information about this scheme, go to www.annesspublishing.com/trees

Acknowledgements

The publisher and authors would like to thank Scenics Cakes Boards, Colours Direct (020 8441 3082) and the Cloth Store (01293 560943) for supplying props and materials, Braun and Kenwood for the use of their equipment, Stork Cookery Service for the Rich Fruit Cake chart and Jackie Mason for her help.

Notes

Bracketed terms are intended for American readers.

For all recipes, quantities are given in both metric and imperial measures and, where appropriate, in standard cups and spoons. Follow one set of measures, but not a mixture, because they are not interchangeable. Standard spoon and cup measures are level. 1 tsp = 5ml, 1 tbsp = 15ml, 1 cup = 250ml/8fl oz.

Australian standard tablespoons are 20ml. Australian readers should use 3 tsp in place of 1 tbsp for measuring small quantities.

American pints are 16fl oz/2 cups. American readers should use 20fl oz/2.5 cups in place of 1 pint when measuring liquids.

Electric oven temperatures in this book are for conventional ovens. When using a fan oven, the temperature will probably need to be reduced by about 10–20°C/20–40°F. Since ovens vary, you should check with your manufacturer's instruction book for guidance.

Medium (US large) eggs are used unless otherwise stated.

The very young, elderly and those in ill-health or with a compromised immune system are advised against consuming foods that contain raw eggs.

Main front cover image shows Cloth of Roses Cake – for recipe, see page 84

Previously published as part of a larger volume, *Complete Cake Decorating*

PUBLISHER'S NOTE

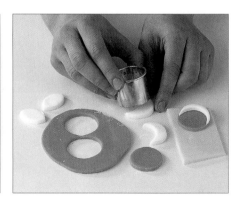

Contents

Introduction

This book is not only an invaluable foundation course in cake-decorating techniques, but also a wonderful reference book for a host of tried-and-tested recipes for classic cake bases and icings, as well as inspirational cake projects, which you will use again and again.

Clearly structured, the decorating course leads you through all the different decorating techniques which can be applied to royal icing, sugarpaste, marzipan, chocolate and other icings. There are step-by-step instructions and photographs for piping, crimping, embossing, frills, plaques, colouring, run-outs, modelling, stencilling, flowers and much more.

The wonderful decorated cakes featured in the Cake Recipes section are a feast for the eye as well as the palate. Moreover, they provide wonderful working examples which you can follow step by step, giving you the opportunity to practise and develop the techniques described in the first section of the book, with professional results.

Within each recipe, three sets of equivalent measurements have been provided: metric, imperial and cups. To avoid disappointing results, never mix the different types of measurement within a recipe. For best results, use eggs which are at room temperature. If you sift flour from a fair height, it will have more chance to aerate and lighten.

No two ovens are alike. If possible, buy a reliable oven thermometer and test the temperature of your oven. Always bake in the centre of the oven where the heat is more likely to be constant. If using a fan assisted oven, follow the manufacturer's guidelines for baking. Good quality cake tins will also improve results, as they conduct heat more efficiently.

Finally, it is important to be aware of the health concerns in regards to the use of raw egg in uncooked recipes. Home-made royal icing, marzipan and sugarpaste icing do include raw egg. An alternative recipe for royal icing, using pure albumen powder, has been provided. If you prefer to avoid raw egg, do buy ready-made marzipan and sugarpaste. Shop-bought versions are usually good quality products and, of course, very quick and easy to use.

$\mathcal{B}$asic Cake Recipes

Cakes are the highlight of many celebrations. What birthday would be complete without a cake with candles to blow out, or a wedding without a beautiful cake to cut? Some of the most traditional cake recipes provide the best bases for decorating. Recipes can be found in this chapter, and are used as bases for the decorated cakes later in the book. None of the cakes involve complicated techniques, and several are as simple as putting the ingredients into a bowl, and mixing them together.

Fruit cake is one of our most popular special occasion cakes. Among its advantages is that it keeps really well and in fact improves with storage, so it can be baked well ahead of time and decorated in easy stages. It also provides a wonderfully firm base for all sorts of elegant or novelty decorations. There are other ideas, too, for those who prefer a less rich tasting cake, such as the Madeira or a light fruit cake, as well as a quick-mix sponge for those last-minute, spontaneous celebrations.

Baking Equipment

A selection of basic equipment is needed for cake making. Here are a few of the more necessary items:

Scales For good, consistent results, ingredients for cake making require precise measuring. An accurate set of scales is therefore essential.

Bowls Various sizes of glass or china heatproof bowls with rounded sides make mixing easier and are useful when baking.

Measuring Jug (Cup) Whether you are working in imperial, metric or cup measurements, a glass measuring jug is easy to read and means liquids are calculated accurately.

Measuring Spoons These are available in a standard size, making the measuring of small amounts more accurate.

Sieves (Strainers) These are used to aerate flour, making cakes lighter, and to remove lumps from icing (confectioners') sugar.

Electric Whisks These whisks are particularly useful for beating egg whites for Swiss rolls.

Balloon Whisks Useful for beating smaller amounts of either egg or cream mixtures.

Baking Parchment Used to line cake tins to prevent cakes from sticking.

Wooden and Metal Spoons Wooden spoons in various sizes are essential

for beating mixtures together when not using an electric mixer, while metal spoons are necessary for folding in ingredients and for smoothing over mixtures to give a flat surface before baking.

Spatulas Because they are so pliable, plastic spatulas are particularly useful for scraping all the cake mixture from a bowl.

Cake Tins (Pans) These are available in all shapes and sizes, and the thicker the metal the less likely the cake will be to overcook. Most cake icing specialists hire out cake tins, useful when very large or unusual shaped tins are required.

Oven Gloves Essential when removing anything hot from the oven. It is worth choosing a good quality, well lined pair of gloves.

Wire Racks Made from wire mesh, these are available in different sizes and shapes and allow cakes to 'breathe' as they cool.

Cake Boards Choose the shape and size to fit the cake. Thick boards are for large, heavy cakes, royal iced cakes and any other fruit cake coated in icing. The board should be 5 cm/2 inches larger than the size of the cake. Thinner boards are for small Madeira cakes and other lighter cakes covered with icings such as butter, glacé or fudge. These can be about 2.5 cm/1 inch larger than the cake size.

1 *glass mixing bowls*
2 *balloon whisk*
3 *large round cake tin (pan)*
4 *electric hand mixer*
5 *small round cake tin (pan)*
6 *scales*
7 *large square cake tin (pan)*
8 *measuring jug (cup)*
9 *measuring spoons*
10 *cake boards*
11 *pastry brush*
12 *pre-cut parchment paper tin (pan) liners*
13 *scissors*
14 *wooden mixing spoons*
15 *wire rack*
16 *sieve (strainer)*
17 *oven gloves*
18 *plastic spatula*
19 *metal spoon*

Quick-mix Sponge Cake

Here's a no-fuss, foolproof all-in-one cake, where the ingredients are quickly mixed together. The following quantities and baking instructions are for a deep 20cm/8 inch round cake tin (pan) or a 20 cm/ 8 inch ring mould. For other quantities and tin sizes, follow the baking instructions given in the decorated cake recipes.

2 ▲ Sift the flour and baking powder into a bowl. Add the margarine, sugar and eggs.

3 ▲ Beat with a wooden spoon for 2–3 minutes. The mixture should be pale in colour and slightly glossy.

INGREDIENTS
115 g/4oz/1 cup self-raising (self-rising) flour
1 tsp baking powder
115 g/4 oz/½ cup soft margarine
115 g/4 oz/½ cup caster (superfine) sugar
2 eggs

STORING AND FREEZING
The cake can be made up to two days in advance, wrapped in clear film (plastic wrap) or foil and stored in an airtight container. The cake can be frozen for up to three months.

FLAVOURINGS
The following amounts are for a 2-egg, single quantity cake, as above. Increase the amounts proportionally for larger cakes.
Chocolate *Fold 1 tbsp cocoa (unsweetened) powder blended with 1 tbsp boiling water into the cake mixture.*
Citrus *Fold 2 tsp of finely grated lemon, orange or lime zest into the cake mixture.*

1 Preheat the oven to 160°C/325°F/ Gas 3. Grease the round cake tin (pan), line the base with greased baking parchment, then grease and flour the ring mould.

4 Spoon the cake mixture into the prepared tin and then smooth the surface. Bake for 20–30 minutes. To test if cooked, press the cake lightly in the centre. If firm, the cake is done, if soft, cook for a little longer. Alternatively, insert a skewer into the centre of the cake. If it comes out clean the cake is ready. Turn out on to a wire rack, remove the baking parchment and leave to cool completely.

This quick-mix sponge cake can be filled and simply decorated with icing for a special occasion.

Swiss Roll

Swiss rolls are traditionally made without fat, so they don't keep as long as most other cakes. However, they have a deliciously light texture and provide the cook with the potential for all sorts of luscious fillings and tasty toppings.

INGREDIENTS
4 eggs, separated
115 g/4 oz/½ cup caster (superfine) sugar
115 g/4 oz/1 cup plain (all-purpose) flour
1 tsp baking powder

STORING AND FREEZING
Swiss rolls and other fat-free sponges do not keep well, so if possible bake on the day of eating. Otherwise, wrap in clear film (plastic wrap) or foil and store in an airtight container overnight or freeze for up to three months.

1 Preheat the oven to 180°C/350°F/ Gas 4. Grease a 33 × 23 cm/ 13 × 9 inch Swiss roll tin (pan), line with baking parchment and grease the paper.

2 Whisk the egg whites in a clean, dry bowl until stiff. Beat in 2 tbsp of the sugar.

3 ▲ Place the egg yolks, remaining sugar and 1 tbsp water in a bowl and beat for about 2 minutes until the mixture is pale and leaves a thick trail when the beaters are lifted.

4 ▼ Carefully fold the beaten egg yolks into the egg white mixture with a metal spoon.

5 Sift together the flour and baking powder. Carefully fold the flour mixture into the egg mixture with a metal spoon.

6 ▲ Pour the cake mixture into the prepared tin and then smooth the surface, being careful not to press out any air.

7 Bake in the centre of the oven for 12–15 minutes. To test if cooked, press lightly in the centre. If the cake springs back it is done. It will also start to come away from the edges of the tin.

8 Turn the cake out on to a piece of baking parchment lightly sprinkled with caster sugar. Peel off the lining parchment and cut off any crisp edges of the cake with a sharp knife. Spread with jam, if wished, and roll up, using the baking parchment as a guide. Leave to cool on a wire rack.

Vary the flavour of a traditional Swiss roll by adding a little grated orange, lime or lemon rind to the basic mixture.

Madeira Cake

This fine-textured cake makes a good base for decorating and is therefore a useful alternative to fruit cake, although it will not keep as long. It provides a firmer, longer-lasting base than a Victoria sponge, and can be covered with butter icing, fudge frosting, a thin layer of marzipan or sugarpaste icing. For the ingredients, decide what size and shape of cake you wish to make and then follow the chart shown opposite.

STORING AND FREEZING
The cake can be made up to a week in advance, wrapped in clear film (plastic wrap) or foil and stored in an airtight container. The cake can be frozen for up to three months.

Madeira cake provides a firmer base for icing than a Victoria sponge. It can be covered with a thin layer of sugarpaste, as here, or marzipan, and is a great alternative for anyone who does not like fruit cake.

1 Preheat the oven to 160°C/325°F/ Gas 3. Grease a deep cake tin (pan), line the base and sides with a double thickness of baking parchment and grease the parchment.

2 ▲ Sift together the flour and baking powder into a mixing bowl. Add the margarine, sugar, eggs and lemon juice.

3 ▲ Stir the ingredients together with a wooden spoon until they are all well combined.

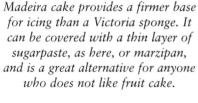

4 ▲ Beat the mixture for about 2 minutes until smooth and glossy.

5 Spoon the mixture into the prepared tin and smooth the top. Bake in the centre of the oven, following the chart opposite as a guide for baking times. If the cake browns too quickly, cover the top loosely with foil. To test if baked, press lightly in the centre. If the cake springs back it is done. Alternatively, test by inserting a skewer into the centre of the cake. If it comes out clean the cake is done. Leave the cake to cool in the tin for 5 minutes and then turn out on to a wire rack. Remove the baking parchment and leave to cool.

MADEIRA CAKE CHART

Cake tin (pan) sizes	18 cm/7 in round	20 cm/8 in round	23 cm/9 in round	25 cm/10 in round	30 cm/12 in round
	15 cm/6 in square	18 cm/7 in square	20 cm/8 in square	23 cm/9 in square	28 cm/11 in square
Plain (all-purpose) flour	225 g/ 8 oz/ 2 cups	350 g/ 12 oz/ 3 cups	450 g/ 1 lb/ 4 cups	500 g/ 1 lb 2 oz/ 4½ cups	625g/ 1½ lb/ 6 cups
Baking powder	1½ tsp	2 tsp	2½ tsp	1 tbsp	4 tsp
Soft margarine	175 g/ 6 oz/ ¾ cup	250 g/ 9 oz/ 1¼ cups	350 g/ 12 oz/ 1½ cups	400 g/ 14 oz/ 1¾ cups	550g/ 1 lb 3 oz 2¼ cups
Caster (superfine) Sugar	175 g/ 6 oz/ ¾ cup	250 g/ 9 oz/ 1¼ cups	350 g/ 12 oz/ 1½ cups	400 g/ 14 oz/ 1¾ cups	550g/ 1 lb 3 oz/ 2½ cups
Eggs, beaten	3	4	6	7	10
Lemon juice	1 tbsp	1½ tbsp	2 tbsp	2½ tbsp	4 tbsp
Approx. baking time	1¼–1½ hours	1½–1¾ hours	1¾–2 hours	1¾–2 hours	2¼–2¼ hours

A traditional Madeira cake peaks and cracks slightly on the top. For a flat surface on which to ice, simply level the top with a sharp knife.

Rich Fruit Cake

This is the traditional cake mixture for many cakes made for special occasions such as weddings, Christmas, anniversaries and christenings. Make the cake a few weeks before icing, keep it well wrapped and stored in an airtight container and it should mature beautifully. Because of all its rich ingredients, this fruit cake will keep moist and fresh for several months. Follow the ingredients guide in the chart opposite for the size of cake you wish to make.

STORING
When the cake is cold, wrap in a double thickness of baking parchment or foil. Store in an airtight container in a cool dry place where it will keep for several months. During storage, the cake can be unwrapped and the bottom brushed with brandy (about half the amount used in the recipe). Re-wrap before storing again. As the cake keeps so well, there is no need to freeze.

A long-lasting cake which is full of rich flavours.

1 Preheat the oven to 140°C/275°F Gas 1. Grease a deep cake tin (pan), line the base and sides with a double thickness of baking parchment and grease the parchment.

2 ▲ Place all the ingredients in a large mixing bowl.

3 ▲ Stir to combine, then beat throughly with a wooden spoon for 3–6 minutes (depending on size), until well mixed.

4 ▲ Spoon the mixture into the prepared tin and smooth the surface with the back of a wet metal spoon. Make a slight impression in the centre to help prevent the cake from doming.

5 Bake in the centre of the oven. Use the chart opposite as a guide for timing the cake you are baking. Test the cake about 30 minutes before the end of the baking time. If the cake browns too quickly, cover the top loosely with foil. To test if baked, press lightly in the centre. If the cake feels firm and when a skewer inserted in the centre comes out clean, it is done. Test again at intervals if necessary.

6 Leave the cake to cool in the tin. When completely cool, turn out of the tin. The baking parchment can be left on to help keep the cake moist.

Rich Fruit Cake Chart

Cake tin (pan) sizes	15 cm/6 in round	18 cm/7 in round	20 cm/8 in round	23 cm/9 in round	25 cm/10 in round	28 cm/11 in round	30 cm/12 in round	33 cm/13 in round
	13 cm/5 in square	15 cm/6 in square	18 cm/7 in square	20 cm/8 in square	23 cm/9 in square	25 cm/10 in square	28 cm/11 in square	30 cm/12 in square
Currants	200 g/ 7 oz/ 1¼ cups	275 g/ 10 oz/ 1¾ cups	375 g/ 13 oz/ 2¼ cups	450 g/ 1 lb/ 3 cups	575 g/ 1¼ lb/ 3½ cups	675 g/ 1½ lb/ 4½ cups	800 g/ 1¾ lb/ 5¼ cups	900 g/ 2 lb/ 6 cups
Sultanas (golden raisins)	115 g/ 4 oz/ ⅔ cup	200 g/ 7 oz/ 1 cup	250 g/ 9 oz/ 1½ cups	300 g/ 11 oz/ 1¾ cups	375 g/ 13 oz/ 2 cups	450 g/ 1 lb/ 2½ cups	550 g/ 1 lb 3 oz/ 3 cups	625 g/ 1 lb 6 oz/ 3½ cups
Raisins	65 g/ 2½ oz/ ⅓ cup	115 g/ 4 oz/ ⅔ cup	150 g/ 5 oz/ ¾ cup	175 g/ 6 oz/ 1 cup	200 g/ 7 oz/ 1 cup	225 g/ 8 oz/ 1¼ cups	250 g/ 9 oz/ 1½ cups	275 g/ 10 oz/ 1½ cups
Glacé (candied) cherries, halved	40 g/ 1½ oz/ ¼ cup	65 g/ 2½ oz/ ⅓ cup	90 g/ 3½ oz/ ½ cup	115 g/ 4 oz/ ½ cup	150 g/ 5 oz/ ⅔ cup	175 g/ 6 oz/ ¾ cup	200 g/ 7 oz/ 1 cup	225 g/ 8 oz/ 1¼ cups
Almonds, chopped	40 g/ 1½ oz/ ⅓ cup	65 g/ 2½ oz/ ½ cup	90 g/ 3½ oz/ ¾ cup	115 g/ 4 oz/ 1 cup	150 g/ 5 oz/ 1¼ cups	175 g/ 6 oz/ 1½ cups	200 g/ 7 oz/ 1⅔ cups	225 g/ 8 oz/ 2 cups
Mixed (candied) peel	40 g/ 1½ oz/ ¼ cup	65 g/ 2½ oz/ ½ cup	65 g/ 2½ oz/ ½ cup	90 g/ 3½ oz/ ⅔ cup	115 g/ 4 oz/ ¾ cup	150 g/ 5 oz/ 1 cup	175 g/ 6 oz/ 1 cup	200 g/ 7 oz/ 1⅓ cups
Lemon, grated rind	½	1	1	2	2	2	3	3
Brandy	1½ tbsp	2 tbsp	2½ tbsp	3 tbsp	3½ tbsp	4 tbsp	4½ tbsp	5 tbsp
Plain (all-purpose) flour	150 g/ 5 oz/ 1⅓ cups	200 g/ 7 oz/ 1¾ cups	250 g/ 9 oz/ 2 cups	300 g/ 11 oz/ 2¾ cups	400 g/ 14 oz/ 3½ cups	450 g/ 1 lb/ 4 cups	550 g/ 1 lb 3 oz/ 4½ cups	625 g/ 1 lb 6 oz/ 5½ cups
Mixed (apple pie) spice	1 tsp	1 tsp	1¼ tsp	1½ tsp	1½ tsp	2 tsp	2½ tsp	1 tbsp
Nutmeg, freshly grated	¼ tsp	½ tsp	½ tsp	1 tsp	1 tsp	1 tsp	1½ tsp	2 tsp
Ground almonds	40 g/ 1½ oz/ ½ cup	50 g/ 2 oz/ ⅔ cup	65 g/ 2½ oz/ ¾ cup	75 g/ 3 oz/ 1 cup	90 g/ 3½ oz/ 1¼ cups	115 g/ 4 oz/ 1⅓ cups	130 g/ 4½ oz/ 1½ cups	150 g/ 5 oz/ 1⅔ cups
Soft margarine or butter	115 g/ 4 oz/ ½ cup	150 g/ 5 oz/ ⅔ cup	200 g/ 7 oz/ scant 1 cup	250 g/ 9 oz/ scant 1¼ cups	300 g/ 11 oz/ scant 1½ cups	375 g/ 13 oz/ scant 1¾ cups	425 g/ 15 oz/ scant 2 cups	500 g/ 1 lb 2 oz/ 2¼ cups
Soft brown sugar	130 g/ 4½ oz/ ⅔ cup	175 g/ 6 oz/ ¾ cup	225 g/ 8 oz/ 1 cup	275 g/ 10 oz/ 1⅓ cups	350 g/ 12 oz/ 1½ cups	400 g/ 14 oz/ scant 2 cups	450 g/ 1 lb/ 2 cups	500 g/ 1 lb 2 oz/ 2¼ cups
Black treacle or molasses	1 tbsp	1 tbsp	1 tbsp	1½ tbsp	2 tbsp	2 tbsp	2 tbsp	2½ tbsp
Eggs, beaten	3	4	5	6	7	8	9	10
Approx. baking time	2¼–2½ hours	2½–2¾ hours	3–3½ hours	3¼–3¾ hours	3¾–4¼ hours	4–4½ hours	4½–5¼ hours	5¼–5¾ hours

Light Fruit Cake

For those who prefer a lighter fruit cake, here is a less rich version, still ideal for marzipanning and covering with sugarpaste or royal icing. Follow the ingredients guide in the chart opposite according to the size of cake you wish to make.

STORING AND FREEZING
When the cake is cold, wrap well in baking parchment, clear film (plastic wrap) or foil. It will keep for several weeks, stored in an airtight container. As the cake keeps so well, there is no need to freeze, but, if wished, freeze for up to three months.

1 Preheat the oven to 150°C/300°F/ Gas 2. Grease a deep cake tin (pan), line the sides and base with a double thickness of baking parchment and grease the parchment.

2 ▲ Measure and prepare all the ingredients, then place them all together in a large mixing bowl.

3 ▲ Stir to combine, then beat thoroughly with a wooden spoon for 3–4 minutes, depending on the size, until well mixed.

4 ▲ Spoon the mixture into the prepared tin and smooth the surface with the back of a wet metal spoon. Make a slight impression in the centre to help prevent the cake from doming.

5 Bake in the centre of the oven. Use the chart opposite as a guide according to the size of cake you are baking. Test the cake about 15 minutes before the end of the baking time. If the cake browns too quickly, cover the top loosely with foil. To test if baked, press lightly in the centre. If the cake feels firm, and when a skewer inserted in the centre comes out clean, it is done. Test again at intervals if necessary.

6 Leave the cake to cool in the tin. When completely cool, turn out of the tin. The baking parchment can be left on to help keep the cake moist.

Round, square, ring or heart-shaped – the shape of this light fruit cake can be varied to suit the occasion.

Light Fruit Cake Chart

	15 cm/6 in round	18 cm/7 in round	20 cm/8 in round	23 cm/9 in round
Cake tin (pan) sizes	13 cm/5 in square	15 cm/6 in square	18 cm/7 in square	20 cm/8 in square
Soft margarine or butter	115 g/ 4 oz/ ½ cup	175 g/ 6 oz/ ¾ cup	225 g/ 8 oz/ 1 cup	275 g/ 10 oz/ 1⅓ cups
Caster (superfine) sugar	115 g/ 4 oz/ ½ cup	175 g/ 6 oz/ ¾ cup	225 g/ 8 oz/ 1 cup	275 g/ 10 oz/ 1⅓ cups
Orange, grated rind	½	½	1	1
Eggs, 3, beaten	3	4	5	6
Plain (all-purpose) flour	165 g 5½ oz/ 1½ cups	200 g/ 7 oz/ 1¾ cups	300 g/ 11 oz/ 2¾ cups	400 g/ 14 oz/ 3½ cups
Baking powder	¼ tsp	½ tsp	½ tsp	1 tsp
Mixed (apple pie) spice	1 tsp	1½ tsp	2 tsp	2½ tsp
Currants	50 g/ 2 oz/ ⅓ cup	115 g/ 4 oz/ ⅔ cup	175 g/ 6 oz/ 1 cup	225 g/ 8 oz/ 1½ cups
Sultanas (golden raisins)	50 g/ 2 oz/ ⅓ cup	115 g/ 4 oz/ ⅔ cup	175 g/ 6 oz/ 1 cup	225 g/ 8 oz/ 1⅓ cups
Raisins	50 g/ 2 oz/ ⅓ cup	115 g/ 4 oz/ ⅔ cup	175 g/ 6 oz/ 1 cup	225 g/ 8 oz/ 1⅓ cups
Dried apricots, chopped	25 g/ 1 oz/ 7	50 g/ 2 oz/ 14	50 g/ 2 oz/ 14	75 g/ 3 oz/ 21
Mixed (candied) peel	50 g/ 2 oz/ scant ½ cup	75 g/ 3 oz/ good ½ cup	115 g/ 4 oz/ ¾ cup	150 g/ 5 oz/ 1 cup
Approx. baking time	2¼ – 2½ hours	2½ – 2¾ hours	2¾ – 3¼ hours	3¼ – 3¾ hours

LINING CAKE TINS

Baking parchment is normally used for lining cake tins. The parchment prevents the cakes from sticking to the tins and makes them easier to turn out. Different cake recipes require slightly different techniques of lining, depending on the shape of the tin, the type of cake mixture, and how long the cake needs to cook. Quick-mix sponge cakes require only one layer of paper to line the base, for example, whereas rich fruit cakes that often bake for several hours if they are large in size need to be lined with a double layer of parchment on the base and sides. This extra protection also helps cakes to cook evenly.

Lining a shallow round tin

This technique is used for a quick-mix sponge cake.

1 Put the tin on a piece of baking parchment and draw around the base of the tin (pan). Cut out the circle just inside the marked line.

2 ▲ Lightly brush the inside of the tin with a little vegetable oil and position the baking parchment circle in the base of the tin. Brush the baking parchment with a little more vegetable oil.

Tip

Softened butter or margarine can be used as a greasing agent in place of vegetable oil, if wished.

Lining a Swiss roll tin

1 Put the tin on a piece of baking parchment and draw around the base of the Swiss roll tin (jelly roll pan). Increase the rectangle by 2.5 cm/1 inch on all sides. Cut out this rectangle and snip each corner diagonally down to the original rectangle.

2 ▲ Lightly brush the inside of the tin with a little vegetable oil and fit the baking parchment into the tin, overlapping the corners slightly so that they fit neatly. Brush the parchment with a little more vegetable oil.

Lining a deep round cake tin

This technique should be used for both rich and light fruit cakes, and Madeira cakes.

1 Put the tin on a double thickness of baking parchment and draw around the base. Cut out just inside the line.

2 For the sides of the tin, cut out a double thickness strip of baking parchment that will wrap around the outside of the tin, allowing a slight overlap, and which is 2.5 cm/1 inch taller than the depth of the tin.

3 Fold over 2.5 cm/1 inch along the length of the side lining. Snip the baking parchment along its length, inside the fold, at short intervals.

4 Brush the inside of the tin with vegetable oil. Slip the side lining into the tin so the snipped edge fits into the curve of the base and sits flat.

5 ▲ Position the base lining in the tin and brush the parchment with a little more vegetable oil.

Lining a deep square cake tin

For rich or light fruit cakes, use good quality fixed-base deep cake tins. Ensure that you have the correct size of tin for the quantity of cake mixture.

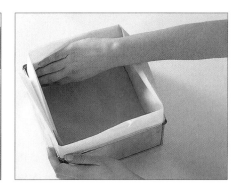

1 Place the tin (pan) on a piece of double thickness waxed paper or baking parchment and draw around the base following the tin shape. Cut out the marked shape with a pair of scissors.

2 Measure and cut a strip of double thickness waxed paper or baking parchment long enough to wrap around the outside of the tin with a small overlap and deep enough to stand 2.5 cm/1 in above the top of the tin.

3 Brush the base and sides of the tin with melted fat or oil. Place the cut-out paper shape in the base of the tin and press flat. Fit the double strip of waxed paper or baking parchment inside the tin, pressing well against the sides and making sharp creases where the paper fits into the corners of the tin. Ensure that the paper strip is level and fits neatly without any creases. Brush the base and sides well with melted fat or oil.

4 Measure and fit a double thickness strip of brown paper around the outside of the tin. Tie it securely with string.

5 Line a baking sheet with several layers of brown paper and stand your prepared cake tin in the centre.

A selection of the different cake tin shapes and sizes available.

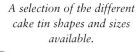

Basic Icing Recipes

Cakes can take on many guises, and nothing enhances their appearance more for that extra special occasion than a little icing. This chapter offers a range of simple classic icing recipes to suit the type of cake you have made and which can be adapted according to the occasion. Ideas range from quick-mix icings, such as butter icing and satin chocolate icing, which may be instantly poured, spread, swirled or piped on to sponge and Madeira cakes or Swiss (jelly) rolls, to the more regal icings, such as royal icing and sugarpaste. These are ideal for covering and decorating fruit cakes intended for more formal occasions, such as anniversaries, christenings and weddings.

The icings in this section are all fairly traditional. However, if you want to substitute any of them with a favourite icing recipe when decorating, make sure that it suits the cake on which you are working.

Decorating Equipment

With a few simple tools, it is possible to create the most stunning of cake decorations. Thick swirls of butter icing formed with a palette knife, or stark white icing sugar dusted over a contrastingly dark (bittersweet) chocolate icing, provides an impressive effect. As your skills develop, however, you will probably want to invest in some specialized pieces of icing equipment, such as those listed here.

Icing Turntable This is one of the most expensive but useful items for either the novice or more advanced cake decorator. Because it revolves, it is particularly handy for piping, or for icing the sides of a round cake with royal icing.

Straight-edge Ruler Choose one made of stainless steel so that it will not bend as you pull it across a layer of royal icing, to give a smooth, flat surface to a cake.

Plastic Scrapers These can have straight or serrated edges for giving a smooth or patterned surface to the sides or tops of cakes coated with royal, butter or fudge icing.

Small Rolling Pin Made in a handy size for rolling out small amounts of marzipan or sugarpaste icing for decorations.

Nozzles There are numerous shapes and sizes to choose from, but it is best to start off with some of the basic shapes. Small straight-sided nozzles fit home-made baking parchment piping (pastry) bags. Larger ones are more suitable for the commercially made material bags when piping large amounts of icing.

Nozzle Brush A small wire brush which makes the job of cleaning out nozzles a lot easier.

Flower Nail Used as a support when piping flowers.

Crimping Tools These are available with different end-shapes which produce varied patterns and offer a quick way of giving a professional finish to a cake.

Paintbrushes Brushes for painting designs on to cakes, adding highlights to flowers or modelled shapes, or for making run-outs are available at cake icing specialists, stationers or art supply shops.

Florist's Wire, Tape and Stamens All available from cake icing specialists, the wire, available in different gauges, is handy for wiring small sugarpaste flowers together to form floral sprays. The tape is used to neaten the stems, and the stamens, available in many colours, form the centres of the flowers.

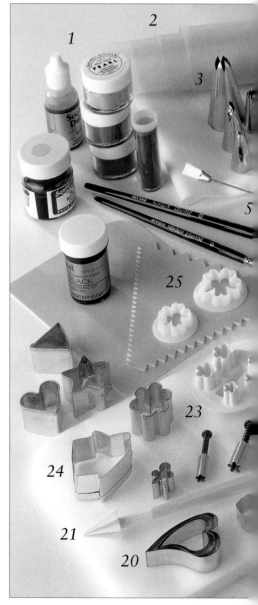

Papers Baking parchment is used for making piping (pastry) bags and for drying sugar-frosted flowers and fruits, and is also used for spreading melted chocolate and for icing run-outs.

Cutters Small cocktail cutters are useful for making cut-out shapes from chocolate, sugarpaste and marzipan. Blossom cutters, available in different shapes and sizes, are good for making small flowers, while a special frill cutter can be used to cut out quick-and-easy frills.

1 *food colourings*
2 *baking parchment*
3 *piping nozzles*
4 *fabric piping (pastry) bag*
5 *nozzle brush*
6 *paintbrushes*
7 *icing turntable*
8 *florist's wire*
9 *stamens*
10 *florist's tape*
11 *straight-edge ruler*
12 *cake pillars*
13 *cake pillar supports*

14 *crimping tools*
15 *food colouring pens*
16 *flower nail*
17 *frill cutter*
18 *textured rolling pin*
19 *foam pad*
20 *shaped cutters*
21 *modelling tool*
22 *plunger cutters*
23 *dual blossom cutter*
24 *cocktail cutters*
25 *plain and serrated side scrapers*

*M*arzipan

With its smooth, pliable texture, marzipan has been popular for centuries in cake making, especially for large cakes such as wedding and christening cakes. It is also excellent for making a variety of cake decorations. The following recipe is sufficient to cover the top and sides of an 18 cm/7 inch round or a 15 cm/6 inch square cake. Make half the amount if only the top is to be covered.

2 ▲ Add the lemon juice, almond extract and enough beaten egg to mix to a soft but firm dough. Gather together with your fingers to form a ball.

3 ▲ Knead the marzipan on a work surface lightly dusted with sifted icing sugar until smooth.

INGREDIENTS
Makes 450 g/1 lb
225 g/8 oz/2¼ cups ground almonds
115 g/4 oz/1 cup icing
(confectioner's) sugar, sifted
115 g/4 oz/½ cup caster
(superfine) sugar
1 tsp lemon juice
2 drops almond extract
1 egg, beaten

STORING
The marzipan will keep for up to four days, wrapped in clear film in an airtight container, and stored in the refrigerator.

1 ▲ Put the ground almonds, icing and caster sugars into a bowl and mix together.

Using Marzipan
Marzipan is applied to the sides and top of a cake, particularly rich fruit cakes, to prevent moisture seeping through the cake and to provide a smooth undercoat for the top covering of royal icing or sugarpaste icing.

Once the marzipan has been applied, leave it to dry for a day or two before applying the icing. For a richer taste you can mix up your own marzipan. However, if you have any concerns about using raw eggs in uncooked recipes, especially in light of current health warnings, do buy ready-made marzipan. It is very good quality, does not contain raw egg and is available in two colours, white and yellow. White is the best choice if you want to add your own colours and create different moulded shapes.

Marzipan can be used as an attractive cake coating in its own right as well as providing a base for other icings.

Sugarpaste Icing

Sugarpaste icing has opened up a whole new concept in cake decorating. It is wonderfully pliable, easy to make and use, and can be coloured, moulded and shaped in the most imaginative fashion. Though quick to make at home, shop-bought sugarpaste, also known as easy-roll or ready-to-roll icing, is very good quality and handy to use. This recipe makes sufficient to cover the top and sides of an 18 cm/7 inch round or a 15 cm/6 inch square cake.

INGREDIENTS
Makes 350 g/12 oz
1 egg white
1 tbsp liquid glucose (clear corn syrup), warmed
350 g/12 oz/3 cups icing (confectioners') sugar, sifted

STORING
The icing will keep for up to a week, wrapped in clear film (plastic wrap) or a plastic bag and stored in the refrigerator. Bring to room temperature before using. If a thin crust forms, trim off before using or it will make the icing lumpy. Also, if the icing dries out or hardens, knead in a little boiled water to make it smooth and pliable again.

1 Put the egg white and glucose in a bowl. Stir together with a wooden spoon to break up the egg white.

2 ▲ Add the icing sugar and mix together with a palette knife or knife, using a chopping action, until well blended and the icing begins to bind together.

3 Knead the mixture with your fingers until it forms a ball.

4 ▲ Knead the sugarpaste on a work surface lightly dusted with sifted icing sugar for several minutes until smooth, soft and pliable. If the icing is too soft, knead in some more sifted icing sugar until it is firm and pliable.

Tip

Ready-made shop-bought sugarpaste does not contain raw egg, so do use if you prefer to avoid uncooked egg in recipes in light of current health warnings.

Tinted or left pure white, sugarpaste icing can be used to cover cakes, and moulded to make decorations to suit any shape of cake.

Royal Icing

Royal icing has gained a regal position in the world of icing. Any special occasion cake which demands a classical, professional finish uses this smooth, satin-like icing. The following recipe makes sufficient to cover the top and sides of an 18 cm/7 inch round or a 15 cm/6 inch square cake.

INGREDIENTS
Makes 675 g/1½ lb
3 size 3 egg whites
about 675 g/1½ lb/6 cups icing (confectioners') sugar, sifted
1½ tsp glycerine
few drops lemon juice
colouring (optional)

STORING
Royal icing will keep for up to three days in an airtight container, stored in the refrigerator. Stir the icing well before using.

Tips

• Always sift the icing sugar before using, to get rid of any lumps.
• Never add more than the stated amount of glycerine. Too much will make the icing crumbly and too fragile to use.
• A little lemon juice is added to prevent the icing from discolouring, but too much will make the icing become hard.

1 ▲ Put the egg whites in a bowl and stir lightly with a wooden spoon to break them up.

2 ▲ Add the icing sugar gradually in small quantities, beating well with a wooden spoon between each addition. Add sufficient icing sugar to make a smooth, white, shiny icing with the consistency of very stiff meringue. It should be thin enough to spread, but thick enough to hold its shape.

3 ▲ Beat in the glycerine, lemon juice and food colouring, if using.

4 It is best to let the icing sit for about 1 hour before using. Cover the surface with a piece of damp clear film (plastic wrap) or a lid so the icing does not dry out. Before using, stir the icing to burst any air bubbles. Even when working with royal icing, always keep it covered.

Royal Icing Using Pure Albumen Powder

If you are concerned about current health warnings advising against the use of raw eggs in uncooked recipes, try the following recipe.

INGREDIENTS
Makes 450 g/1 lb
450 g/1 lb/4 cups icing sugar, (confectioners') sifted
6 tbsp water
12.5g/½ oz/7 tsp pure albumen powder

STORING
This royal icing will keep for up to a week in an airtight container, stored in a cool place.

1 Mix the pure albumen powder with the water. Leave to stand for 15 minutes, then stir until the powder dissolves.

2 Strain the albumen solution into a mixing bowl. Add half the icing sugar and beat until smooth. Add the remaining sugar and beat again for 12–14 minutes or until smooth.

3 Adjust the consistency as needed, adding a little more icing sugar for a stiffer icing or a little water for a thinner one. If storing, transfer to an airtight container, cover the surface of the royal icing with clear film and then close the lid.

ICING CONSISTENCIES

For flat icing

▲ The recipes on the opposite page are for a consistency of icing suitable for flat icing a rich fruit cake covered in marzipan. When the spoon is lifted out of the icing, it should form a sharp point, with a slight curve at the end, known as a 'soft peak'.

For peaking

▲ Make the royal icing as before, but to a stiffer consistency so that when the spoon is lifted out of the bowl the icing stands in straight peaks.

For piping

For piping purposes, the icing needs to be slightly stiffer than for peaked icing so that it forms a fine, sharp peak when the spoon is lifted out. This allows the icing to flow easily for piping, at the same time enabling it to keep its definition.

For run-outs

For elegant and more elaborate cakes, you may want to pipe outlines of shapes and then fill these in with different coloured icing. These are known as run-outs. For the outlines, you need to make the icing to a piping consistency, while for the insides you need a slightly thinner icing with a consistency of thick cream, so that with a little help it will flow within the shapes. Ideally the icing should hold its shape and be slightly rounded after filling the outlines.

The right consistency

If you need to change the consistency of your icing, add a little sifted icing sugar to make it stiffer, or beat in a little egg white for a thinner icing. Be sure to do this carefully, as a little of one or the other will change the consistency fairly quickly.

A traditional look for a classic royal icing. This square rich fruit cake has been marzipanned and then flat iced with three, ultra-smooth layers of royal icing. It is simply, but elegantly, decorated with piped borders, a crisp, white ribbon and fresh roses.

ℬutter Icing

*The creamy, rich flavour and silky smoothness of butter icing are popular with both
children and adults. The icing can be varied in colour and flavour and makes
a decorative filling and coating for sponge and Madeira cakes or Swiss rolls.
Simply swirled, or more elaborately piped, butter icing gives a delicious
and attractive finish. The following quantity makes enough to fill and coat the
sides and top of a 20 cm/8 inch sponge cake.*

2 ▲ Beat with a wooden spoon or an
electric mixer, adding sufficient
extra milk to give a light, smooth and
fluffy consistency.

FLAVOURINGS

*The following amounts are for a
single quantity of icing. Increase or
decrease the amounts proportionally
as needed.*
Chocolate *Blend 1 tbsp unsweetened
cocoa powder with 1 tbsp hot water.
Allow to cool before beating into
the icing.*
Coffee *Blend 2 tsp instant coffee
powder or granules with 1 tbsp
boiling water. Allow to cool before
beating into the icing.*
Lemon, orange or lime *Substitute
the vanilla extract and milk for
lemon, orange or lime juice and
2 tsp of finely grated citrus zest.
Omit the zest if using the icing for
piping. Lightly colour the icing with
the appropriate shade of food
colouring, if wished.*

INGREDIENTS
Makes 350 g/12 oz
*75 g/3 oz/6 tbsp butter, softened,
or soft margarine
225 g/8 oz/2 cups icing
(confectioner's) sugar, sifted
1 tsp vanilla extract
2–3 tsp milk*

STORING
*The icing will keep for up to three
days, in an airtight container stored
in the refrigerator.*

1 ▲ Put the butter or margarine, icing
sugar, vanilla extract and 1 tsp of
the milk in a bowl.

*Generous swirls of butter icing give
a mouthwatering effect to a cake.*

Glacé Icing

*This icing can be made in just a few minutes
and can be varied by adding a few drops of food colouring or
flavouring. The following quantity makes enough to cover the top
and decorate a 20 cm/8 inch round sponge cake.*

INGREDIENTS
Makes 225 g/8 oz
*225 g/8 oz/2 cups icing
(confectioners') sugar
2–3 tbsp warm water or fruit juice
food colouring, optional*

STORING
*Not suitable for storing.
The icing must be used
immediately after making.*

2 ▲ Using a wooden spoon, gradually
stir in enough water to make an
icing with the consistency of thick
cream. Beat until the icing is smooth. It
should be thick enough to coat the back
of the spoon. If it is too runny, beat in a
little more sifted icing sugar.

3 To colour the icing, beat in a few
drops of food colouring. Use the
icing immediately for coating or piping.

1 ▲ Sift the icing sugar into a mixing
bowl to get rid of any lumps.

*Drizzled or spread, glacé icing can
quickly turn a plain cake into
something special.*

Fudge Frosting

A rich, darkly delicious frosting, this can transform a simple sponge cake into one worthy of a very special occasion. Spread fudge frosting smoothly over the cake or swirl it. Or be even more elaborate with a little piping - it is very versatile. The following amount will fill and coat the top and sides of a 20 cm/8 inch or 23 cm/9 inch round sponge cake.

2 ▲ Stir over a very low heat until the chocolate and butter or margarine melt. Remove from the heat and stir until evenly blended.

3 ▲ Beat the icing frequently as it cools until it thickens sufficiently to use for spreading or piping. Use immediately and work quickly once it has reached the right consistency.

INGREDIENTS
Makes 350 g/12 oz
50 g/2 oz plain (semisweet) chocolate
225 g/8 oz/2 cups icing (confectioners') sugar, sifted
50 g/2 oz/4 tbsp butter or margarine
3 tbsp milk or single (light) cream
1 tsp vanilla extract

STORING
Not suitable for storing. The icing must be used immediately after making.

1 ▲ Break or chop the chocolate into small pieces. Put the chocolate, icing sugar, butter, milk and vanilla extract in a heavy pan.

Thick glossy swirls of fudge icing almost make a decoration in themselves on this cake.

Satin Chocolate Icing

Shiny as satin and smooth as silk, this rich chocolate icing can be poured over a sponge cake. A few fresh flowers, pieces of fresh fruit, simple chocolate shapes or white chocolate piping add the finishing touch. Use this recipe to cover a 20 cm/8 inch square or a 23 cm/9inch round quick-mix sponge or Madeira cake.

INGREDIENTS
Makes 225 g/8 oz
175 g/6 oz plain (semisweet) chocolate
150 ml/¼ pint/⅔ cup single (light) cream
½ tsp instant coffee powder

STORING
Not suitable for storing. The icing must be used immediately after making.

Tip

Before using the icing, place the cake on a wire rack positioned over a piece of baking parchment. This will avoid unnecessary mess.

2 ▲ Stir over a very low heat until the chocolate melts and the mixture is smooth and evenly blended.

3 Remove from the heat and immediately pour the icing over the cake, letting it slowly run down the sides to coat it completely. Spread the icing with a palette knife as necessary, working quickly before the icing has time to thicken.

Satin chocolate icing brings a real touch of sophistication to the most humble of cakes.

1 ▲ Break or chop the chocolate into small pieces. Put the chocolate, cream and coffee in a small heavy pan. Place the cake to be iced on a wire rack.

Covering Cakes

Covering cakes with icing – whether marzipan, royal or sugarpaste – not only provides a wonderful surface for decorating but also helps to keep the cake moist. The icings need to be applied with care to ensure that the finish is beautifully smooth. Always plan ahead; it will take several days to marzipan and royal ice a cake, allowing for the drying out times.

Marzipanning a Cake for Sugarpaste Icing

Marzipan can be applied as an icing in its own right, but is mainly used as a base for sugarpaste or royal icing. Unlike a cake covered in royal icing which traditionally has sharp, well defined corners, a cake covered in sugarpaste has much smoother lines with rounded corners and edges. There are therefore two different techniques depending on how you wish to ice the cake.

1 If the cake is not absolutely flat, fill any hollows or build up the top edge (if it is lower than the top of the cake) with a little marzipan. Brush the top of the cake with a little warmed and strained apricot jam.

3 ▲ Lift the marzipan using your hands, or place it over a rolling pin to support it, and position over the top of the cake. Drape the marzipan over the cake to cover it evenly.

5 ▲ With a sharp knife, trim the excess marzipan, cutting it flush with the base of the cake.

2 ▲ Lightly dust a work surface with icing (confectioners') sugar. Knead the marzipan into a smooth ball. Roll out to a 5 mm/¼ inch thickness and large enough to cover the top and sides of the cake, allowing about an extra 7.5 cm/3 inches all around for trimming. Make sure the marzipan does not stick to the work surface and moves freely.

4 ▲ Smooth the top with the palm of your hand to eliminate any air bubbles. Then carefully lift up the edges of the marzipan and let them fall against the sides of the cake, being careful not to stretch the marzipan. Ensure the marzipanned sides are flat and there are no creases – all the excess marzipan should fall on to the work surface. Use the palms of your hands to smooth the sides and eliminate air bubbles.

6 ▲ With your hands, work in a circular motion over the surface of the marzipan to give it a smooth finish. Spread a little royal icing over the middle of a cake board and place the cake in the centre to secure. Lay a piece of baking parchment over the top to protect the surface, then leave for at least 12 hours to dry before covering with icing.

Marzipanning a Round Cake for Royal Icing

1 ▲ If the cake is not absolutely flat, fill any hollows or build up the top edge (if it is lower than the top of the cake) with a little marzipan.

2 Brush the top of the cake with warmed and strained apricot jam.

3 Lightly dust a work surface with icing (confectioners') sugar. Using one-third of the marzipan, knead it into a ball. Roll out to a round 5 mm/¼ inch thickness and 1 cm/½ inch larger than the top of the cake. Make sure that the marzipan does not stick to the work surface and moves freely.

4 ▲ Invert the top of the cake on to the marzipan. Trim the marzipan almost to the edge of the cake. With a small metal palette knife, press the marzipan inwards so it is flush with the edge of the cake.

▶ The method for marzipanning a square cake for royal icing is the same as for a round one, except for the sides. Measure the length and height of the sides with string and roll out the marzipan in four separate pieces, using the string measurements as a guide.

5 Carefully turn the cake the right way up. Check the sides of the cake. If there are any holes, fill them with marzipan to make a flat surface. Brush the sides with apricot jam.

6 Knead the remaining marzipan and any trimmings (making sure there are no cake crumbs on the work surface) to form a ball. For the sides of the cake, measure the circumference with a piece of string, and the height of the sides with another piece.

7 ▲ Roll out a strip of marzipan to the same thickness as the top, matching the length and width to the measured string. Hold the cake on its side, being careful to touch the marzipanned top as lightly as possible. Roll the cake along the marzipan strip, pressing the marzipan into position to cover the sides. Trim if necessary to fit.

8 ▲ Smooth the joins together with a metal spatula. Spread a little royal icing into the middle of a cake board and place the cake in the centre to secure. Lay a piece of baking parchment very loosely over the top to protect the surface, then leave for at least 24 hours to dry before covering with icing.

Tip

When buying marzipan, it is best to choose the white kind for covering a cake, as the bright yellow marzipan may discolour pale coloured sugarpaste or royal icing.

Covering a Round Cake with Royal Icing

A cake which is coated with royal icing is always covered with marzipan first. The marzipan should be applied one to two days before the royal icing so it has time to dry out slightly, giving a firm surface on which to work. The royal icing is then built up in two or three layers, each one being allowed to dry out before covering with the next. The final coat should be perfectly flat and smooth, with no air bubbles.

Tip

It is difficult to calculate the exact amount of icing required, but if you work with 450g/1lb/⅔ quantity batches, it should always be fresh. While working, keep the royal icing in a bowl and cover with a clean, damp cloth or clear film (plastic wrap) so it does not dry out.

1 The icing should be of 'soft peak' consistency. Put about 2 tbsp of icing in the centre of the marzipanned cake (the amount will depend on the size of cake you are icing).

2 ▲ Using a small palette knife, spread the icing over the top of the cake, working back and forth with the flat of the knife to eliminate any air bubbles. Keep working the icing in this way until the top of the cake is completely covered. Trim any icing that extends over the edge of the cake with the palette knife.

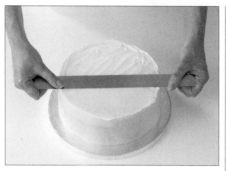

3 ▲ Position a straight-edge ruler on the top edge of the cake furthest away from you. Slowly and smoothly pull the ruler across the surface of the icing, holding it at a slight angle. Do this without stopping to prevent ridges forming. You may need several attempts to get a smooth layer, in which case simply re-spread the top of the cake with icing and try again.

4 ▲ Trim any excess icing from the top edges of the cake with the palette knife to give a straight, neat edge. Leave the icing to dry for several hours, or overnight, in a dry place before continuing.

5 ▲ Place the cake on a turntable. To cover the sides, spread some icing on to the side of the cake with a palette knife. Rock the knife back and forth as you spread the icing to eliminate air bubbles. Rotate the turntable as you work your way around the cake.

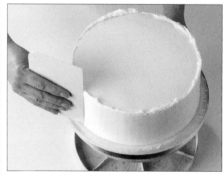

6 ▲ Using a plain side-scraper, hold it firmly in one hand against the side of the cake at a slight angle. Turn the turntable round in a continuous motion and in one direction with the other hand, while pulling the scraper smoothly in the opposite direction to give a smooth surface to the iced sides. When you have completed the full turn, carefully lift off the scraper to leave a neat join. Trim off any excess icing from the top edge and the cake board.

7 Leave the cake to dry, uncovered, then apply the icing in the same way to give the cake two or three more coats of icing. For a really smooth final layer, use a slightly softer consistency of icing.

Covering a Square Cake

The method is essentially the same as for icing a round cake.

1 Cover the top with icing as for the round cake. Leave to dry.

2 ▲ Cover the sides as for the round cake, but work on one side at a time and allow the icing to dry out before continuing with the next side. You will not need a turntable. Simply pull the scraper firmly and smoothly across each side in a single movement, repeating if necessary, for a really smooth finish.

3 ▲ Trim off any excess icing from the cake board with a knife.

4 Leave the cake to dry, uncovered, then apply the icing in the same way to give the cake two or three more coats of icing. For a really smooth final layer, use a slightly softer consistency.

This Christmas Tree cake shows a version of peaked, or rough, icing. The fruit cake is first covered with coloured marzipan and left to dry for 12 hours, then royal icing is peaked around the lower half of the sides. The colour decorations are also made of coloured marzipan.

Rough Icing a Cake

Peaking the icing to give it a rough appearance, like that of snow, is a much quicker and simpler way of applying royal icing to a cake. It is also much quicker to apply as you only need one covering of icing.

1 ▲ Spread the icing evenly over the cake, bringing the icing right to the edges so the cake is completely covered.

2 ▲ Starting at the bottom of the cake, press the flat side of a palette knife into the icing, then pull away sharply to form a peak. Repeat until the whole cake is covered with peaks. Alternatively, flat ice the top of the cake and rough ice the sides – or vice versa.

Covering with Sugarpaste Icing

Sugarpaste icing is a quick, professional way to cover a cake. Although fruit cakes are usually covered with marzipan first, this is not necessary if you are using a sponge base. The sugarpaste can be applied in one coating, unlike royal icing which requires several coats for a really smooth finish. Keep the icing white or knead in a little food colouring to tint. Ready-made sugarpaste is extremely good quality and is available in various colours for fast and professional results.

1 Carefully brush a little water or sherry over the marzipanned surface to help the icing stick to the marzipan. (If you miss a patch, unsightly air bubbles may form.)

2 ▲ Lightly dust a work surface with icing sugar. Roll out the sugarpaste to a 5 mm/¼ inch thickness and large enough to cover the top and sides of the cake plus a little extra for trimming. Make sure the icing does not stick to the surface and moves freely.

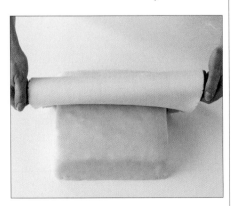

3 ▲ Lift the sugarpaste using your hands, or place it over a rolling pin to support it, and position over the top of the cake. Drape the sugarpaste over the cake to cover it evenly.

4 ▲ Dust your hands with a little cornflour. Smooth the top and sides of the cake with your hands, working from top to bottom, to eliminate any air bubbles.

5 ▲ With a sharp knife, trim off the excess sugarpaste, cutting flush with the base of the cake.

6 Spread a little royal icing into the middle of a cake board and place the cake in the centre to secure.

Tip

To avoid damaging the surface of the cake while you move it, slide the cake to the edge of the work surface and support it underneath with your hand. Lift it and place on the cake board.

Covering Awkward Shapes

Although most shapes of cake can be covered smoothly with one piece of sugarpaste icing, there are some which need to be covered in sections. A cake baked in a ring mould is one such. The top and outer side of the cake is covered with two identical pieces of sugarpaste, and the inner side with a third piece.

1 ▲ Measure half of the outer circumference of the cake with a piece of string, then measure the side and rounded top with another piece of string.

2 ▲ Take three-quarters of the sugarpaste icing and cut in half. Keep the remaining icing well wrapped until needed. Brush the marzipan lightly with water. Roll out each half of the icing into a rectangle, matching the string measurements. Cover the top and side of the cake in two halves.

3 Measure the circumference and the height of the inner side with two pieces of string. Roll out the reserved sugarpaste icing into a rectangle matching the string measurements, and use to cover the inside of the ring. Trim the sugarpaste to fit and press the joins together securely.

FOOD COLOURINGS & TINTS

Food colourings and tints for cake making are available today in almost as large a range as those found on an artist's palette. This has opened up endless possibilities for the cake decorator to create the most imaginative and colourful designs. Liquid colours are only suitable for marzipan and sugarpaste icing if a few drops are required to tint the icing a very pale shade. If used in large amounts they will soften the icings too much. So for vibrant, stronger colours, as well as for subtle sparkling tints, use pastes or powders, available from cake icing specialists. When choosing colours for icings, ensure that they are harmonious, and complement your design.

Colouring icings

How you apply the colour to an icing depends on whether it is in liquid form, a paste or powder. While working with the colourings it is best to stand them on a plate or washable board so they do not mark your work surface. When using cocktail sticks for transferring the colour to the icing, select a fresh stick for each colour so the colours do not become mixed.

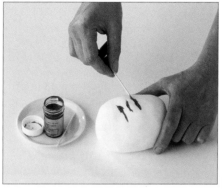

2 ▲ To colour firmer icings, such as sugarpaste and marzipan, use paste colourings. Dip a cocktail stick (toothpick) into the colouring and streak it on to the surface of a ball of the icing.

4 ▲ To create subtle tints in specific areas, brush powdered colourings on to the surface of the icing.

1 ▲ Add liquid colour to the icing a few drops at a time until the required shade is reached. Stir into softer icings, such as butter, royal or glacé.

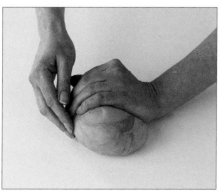

3 ▲ Knead thoroughly until the colour is evenly worked in and there is no streaking. Add sparingly at first, remembering that the colour becomes more intense as the icing stands, then leave for about 10 minutes to see if it is the shade you need.

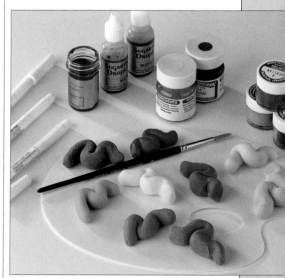

A cake decorator's palette – a vivid array of food colourings to help bring out the artist in you.

Decorating with Royal Icing

Of all the icings, royal icing is probably the most complex and hardest to work with. But once the techniques are mastered, it provides a classic backdrop for both traditional as well as more contemporary cake designs. Traditionally it is used for decorating white wedding and Christmas cakes, but as colour is being introduced more and more into cake decorating, royal icing can now be used in many imaginative ways. This chapter demonstrates how to introduce a modern look using a wide variety of classic techniques.

Making and Using Piping (Pastry) Bags

A piping bag is an essential tool when working with royal icing. You can buy piping bags made of washable fabric and icing syringes, which are ideal for the beginner or for piping butter icing in bold designs. However, for more intricate piping, particularly if using several icing colours and nozzles, home-made greaseproof paper or baking parchment piping bags are more practical and flexible to handle. Make up several ahead of time, following the instructions given here, then fit them with straight-sided nozzles. Do not use nozzles with ridges as they do not have such a tight fit in the bag. To prevent the icing drying out when working with several bags, cover the nozzle ends with a damp cloth when not in use.

2 ▶ With the point of the triangle facing away from you, hold the triangle with your thumb in the middle of the longest edge. Take the left corner and bring it over to meet the point of the triangle, as shown.

3 ▼ Hold in position and bring the remaining corner round and back over to meet the other two points, forming a cone shape. Holding all the points together, position them to make the cone tight and the point of it sharp, as shown.

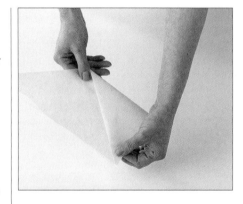

1 ▲ Cut out a 25 cm/10 inch square of baking parchment. Fold it in half diagonally to make a triangle.

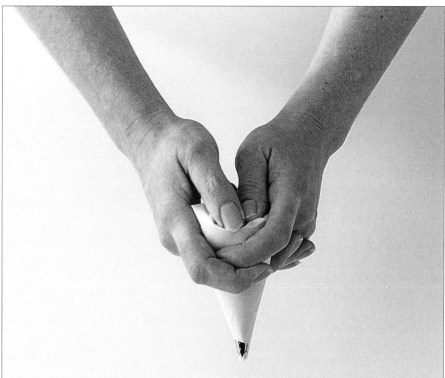

4 ▲ With the cone open, turn the points neatly inside the top edge, creasing firmly down. Secure the cone with a staple.

5 For using with a nozzle, cut off the pointed end of the bag and position the nozzle so it fits snugly into the point. Half-fill the bag with icing and fold over the top to seal. To use without a nozzle, add the icing, seal, then cut a small straight piece off the end of the bag to pipe lines.

6 For ease and control, it is important to hold the bag in a relaxed position. You may find it easier to hold it with one or both hands. For one hand, hold the bag between your middle and index fingers and push out the icing with your thumb.

7 ▲ If using both hands, simply wrap the other hand around the bag in the same manner, so both thumbs can push the icing out.

8 ▲ To pipe, hold the bag so the nozzle is directly over the area you want to pipe on. The bag will be held straight or at an angle, depending on the shape you are piping. Gently press down with your thumb on the top of the bag to release the icing, and lift your thumb to stop the flow of icing. Use a small metal spatula to cut off any excess icing from the tip of the nozzle as you lift the bag from each piped shape, to keep the shapes neat.

Royal icing is the perfect icing for piping. This cake shows how you can achieve pretty effects with shells, stars, lines and beads. Piped roses in full bloom complement the colour chosen for the top of the cake, and the petal tips have been highlighted with food colouring. Carry the design on to the cake board for a classic celebratory cake.

Piping Shapes

Royal icing gives cakes a professional finish, and is often used in decorating to give a formal and ornate character to a cake. However, simple piping skills can easily be achieved given a little practice. This section shows you how, with just a few piping nozzles, you can enhance the look of your cakes. Remember that the icing must be of the correct consistency – not too firm or it will be difficult to squeeze out of the piping (pastry) bag, and not too soft or the piping will not hold its shape. Small nozzles are used for the delicate designs made with royal icing. Larger ones are more suitable for butter icing and frostings.

Piping Twisted Ropes and Leaves

For the ropes, fit nozzles Nos 43 or 44, or a writing nozzle, into a baking parchment piping bag and half-fill with icing. Hold the bag at a slight angle and pipe in a continuous line with even pressure, twisting the bag as you pipe. For leaves, you can use a No 18 petal nozzle or simply cut off the point of the bag in the shape of an arrow. Place the tip of the bag on the cake, holding the bag at a slight angle. Pipe out the icing, then pull away quickly to make the tapering end of a leaf.

Twisted ropes and leaves

Stars, swirls and scrolls

Piping Stars

For a simple star shape, choose a star-shaped nozzle in a size to suit your design. Hold the piping bag upright directly over the area to be iced. Gently squeeze the bag to release the icing and to form a star. Pull off quickly and sharply, keeping the bag straight, to give a neat point to the star.

Piping Swirls

Choose a star-shaped nozzle in a size to suit your design. Hold the piping bag directly over the area to be iced. Pipe a swirl in a circular movement, then pull off quickly and sharply, keeping the bag straight to leave a neat point.

Piping Scrolls

Choose star or rope nozzles in a size to suit your design. Hold the piping bag at a slight angle and place the tip of the nozzle on the cake. Pipe the icing lightly upwards and outwards, then come down in a circular movement, tailing off the icing so the end rests on the cake to make a scroll. The action is a little like piping a large 'comma'. For a reverse scroll, repeat as before, but pipe in the opposite direction, going inwards to reverse the shape. A scroll border can be particularly effective if you alternate two colours of icing.

Piping Cornelli

Cornelli is a fun technique which can be carried out in one or more colours. It is a little like doodling. Use writing nozzles Nos 1 or 2 and pipe a continuous flow of icing, squiggling the lines in the shape of W's and M's.

Piping Simple Embroidery

Piped embroidery is very fine work, requiring writing nozzles Nos 0 or 1. Keep the design simple and work in one or several colours. Pipe little circles, lines and dots to make a delicate pattern for your cake. Look at textile embroidery designs for some ideas.

Cornelli and simple embroidery

Piping Dots or Beads

Use writing nozzles Nos 1, 2 or 3. Hold the piping (pastry) bag directly over the area you wish to pipe. Press out the icing so it forms a bead, then release the pres-sure on the bag and take it off gently to one side. The smaller size nozzle will make simple dots. Neither dots nor beads should end in a sharp point. If this happens, lightly press any sharp points back into the bead with a small damp brush, or try making the icing a little softer.

Piping Shells

Use star nozzles Nos 5 or 8. Rest the tip of the nozzle on the cake and pipe out a little icing to secure it to the surface. Gently squeeze out the icing while lifting the bag slightly up and then down, ending with the nozzle back on the surface of the cake. Pull off to release the icing. Repeat, allowing the beginning of the next shell to touch the end of the first one and continue in this way until you have completed a continuous line of shells.

Piping Lines

Use a writing nozzle, remembering that the smaller the hole, the finer the line. Hold the bag at an angle, rest the nozzle on the cake and pipe out a little icing to secure it to the surface. Pipe the icing, lifting the bag slightly as you work, so it is just above the surface of the cake. Continue to pipe, allowing the line of piping to fall in a straight line. Do not pull or the line will break. At the end of the line, release the pressure, rest the nozzle on the surface of the cake and pull off to break the icing. The line can be varied by curving or looping it.

Piping Trellises

To pipe trellises, use the same technique as above to pipe a set of parallel lines. Then overpipe a set in the opposite direction for squares, or horizontally across the lines for diamonds. You can also get different effects by using different widths of writing nozzles.

Piping Zigzags

Use a No 2 or 3 writing nozzle and pipe either one continuous zigzag, or stop and start at the end of each point to make them sharper.

Dots and beads

Lines, trellises and zigzags

Shells

Piped Sugar Pieces

These little piped sugar pieces are very fragile and have the appearance of fine lace. They must be made ahead of time, and left to dry. The sugar pieces need to be handled carefully, and it is a good idea to make plenty in case of breakages.

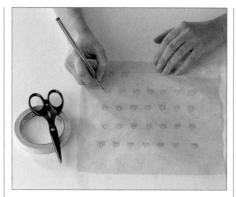

1 ▲ On a piece of baking parchment, draw your chosen design several times with pencil. The designs should be kept fairly small.

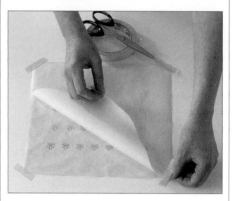

2 ▲ Tape the paper to the work surface or a flat board and secure a piece of baking parchment over the top. Tape the baking parchment down at the corners with masking tape.

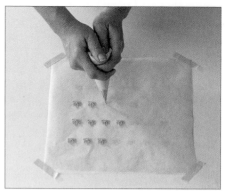

3 ▲ Fit a piping (pastry) bag with a No 1 writing nozzle. Half-fill with royal icing, and fold over the top to seal. Pipe over each design, carefully following the pencilled lines with a continuous thread of icing. Repeat, piping as many pieces as you need plus a few extra in case of any breakages.

4 Leave to dry for at least two hours. Remove from the paper by carefully turning it back and lifting off each piece with a metal spatula. When dry, store in a box between layers of tissue paper.

Shapely forms – delicate piped sugar pieces can be made in all kinds of designs and colours and attached to the sides, tops or edges of cakes with a dab of royal icing.

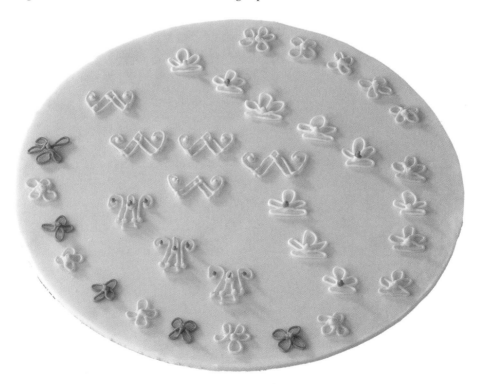

Simple Piped Flowers

To make these pretty piped flowers, you will need a petal nozzle – either small, medium or large depending on how big you want the flowers to be – a paper piping (pastry) bag, a cocktail stick (toothpick) and a flower nail. Make the flowers ahead of time and, when dry, store in a box between layers of tissue paper.

ROSE

1 For a tightly formed rose, make a fairly firm icing. Colour the icing, or leave it white. Fit the petal nozzle into a paper piping (pastry) bag, half-fill with royal icing and fold over the top to seal.

2 Hold the piping bag so the wider end of the nozzle is pointing into what will be the base of the flower, and hold a cocktail stick in the other hand. Pipe a small cone shape around the tip of a cocktail stick. Pipe a petal half way around the cone, lifting it so it is at an angle and curling outwards, not flat, and turning the cocktail stick at the same time.

3 ▲ Repeat with more petals so they overlap each other slightly. The last petals can lie flatter and be more open. Remove the rose from the cocktail stick by threading the stick through a large hole on a grater. The rose will rest on the grater. Leave until dry and firm.

PANSY

1 Colour the icing. Fit the petal nozzle into a paper piping (pastry) bag, half-fill with royal icing and fold over the top to seal. Cut out a small square of baking parchment and secure to the flower nail with a little icing.

2 ▲ Holding the nozzle flat, pipe the petal shape in a curve, turning the flower nail at the same time. Pipe five petals in all. Pipe beads of yellow icing in the centre with a small writing nozzle, or use stamens.

3 Remove the baking parchment from the flower nail, but leave the pansy on the paper until it is dry and firm. Coloured details can be added by painting with food colouring, or using food colouring pens, once the flower has dried. Lift the pansy from the baking parchment by carefully slipping a metal spatula underneath the base of the flower.

COLOURED SUMMER FLOWERS

1 Colour the icing. Make up the flowers in a variety of shades for a colourful arrangement. Fit the petal nozzle into a paper piping (pastry) bag, half-fill with royal icing and fold over the top to seal. Cut out a small square of baking parchment and secure to the flower nail with a little icing.

2 ▲ Pipe five flat petals in a circle so they slightly overlap each other. Pipe beads of yellow icing in the centre of each flower or sprinkle with hundreds and thousands. Leave to dry and add coloured details as for the pansy.

Bouquet of iced blossoms, including roses, pansies and bright summer flowers – arrangements of piped flowers make colourful cake decorations.

Decorating with Sugarpaste Icing

As a covering, sugarpaste icing gives a softer look to a cake than royal icing. It is much quicker to work with, requiring only one rolled out layer. This is then placed in position so it curves itself over the edges of the cake. Because it is so pliable, sugarpaste can also be used for a wide range of decorative effects. When making sugarpaste decorations, always wrap any icing you are not using immediately in clear film (plastic wrap) to stop it drying out.

Marbling

As an alternative to covering a cake in a single colour, sugarpaste icing can be marbled for a multi-coloured effect. Use several colours and keep them quite vibrant, or use one or two delicate tones. Marbled sugarpaste icing can also be used to make effective moulded flowers and other modelled decorations.

1 ▲ Form the sugarpaste icing into a smooth roll or ball. Dip the end of a cocktail stick into the food colouring and dab a few drops on to the icing. Repeat with more colours if wished.

2 ▲ Knead the sugarpaste icing just a few times. The colouring should look very patchy.

3 ▲ On a work surface lightly sprinkled with icing (confectioners') sugar, roll out the sugarpaste icing to reveal the marbled effect.

4 ▲ Alternatively, for a very bold interweaving of colours, use the following technique. Divide the sugarpaste icing into three or four equal portions, depending on how many colours you want to use. Colour them with food colouring. Divide each colour into four or five portions and roll out with your hands into sausage shapes. If you like, you could even put two colours together to make an instant marbled sausage. Place the different-coloured sausages side-by-side on the work surface.

5 ▲ Twist the colours together and knead for several seconds until the strips of colour are fused together but retain their individual colours.

6 ▲ Roll out the marbled icing on a work surface lightly dusted with icing sugar.

Crimping

Crimping tools are similar to large tweezers with patterned ends and are available in a good variety of styles. Crimping is a very quick and efficient way of giving decorative edges and borders to sugarpaste-coated cakes – the effect is similar to the embroidery technique of smocking. For a simple finish to the crimped cake, top with a small posy of edible flowers, a ribbon, or other bought decorations.

1 ▲ Cover the cake with sugarpaste icing. For crimping, the icing must still be soft, so do not allow it to dry out before decorating. Dip the crimping tool in a little cornflour (cornstarch).

2 ▼ Position the crimping tool on the cake in the place you wish to start the design and squeeze the teeth together to make the pattern.

3 ▲ Slowly release the crimper so as not to tear the icing. Repeat the pattern, either touching the last one or spacing them evenly apart. The pattern can be varied by using different crimping tools.

4 ▲ The same technique can be used to crimp decorative designs down the sides of a cake. If applying sugarpaste frills to a cake, crimp the edges for a neat and pretty finish.

Embossing

Special embossing tools can be purchased from cake icing specialists, but you can also use any other patterned items such as cookie stamps, cutters or icing nozzles.

1 ▲ Cover the cake with sugarpaste icing. For embossing, the icing must still be soft, so do not allow it to dry out. Brush a little cornflour (cornstarch) on to the embossing tool and press firmly on to the soft icing. Repeat, brushing with cornflour each time.

2 ▲ To add colour, brush a little powdered food colouring on to the embossing tool instead of the cornflour and press on to the icing as before. Highlights can also be added with food colouring pens, as shown.

3 ▲ Textured rolling pins are also available from cake icing specialists. Cover the cake with sugarpaste icing as before and smooth over with your hand. Roll over the surface of the icing with the textured rolling pin. This rolling pin gives a basketweave effect.

ecorating with Marzipan

Marzipan can be a decorative icing in its own right, or it can provide a firm undercoat for a royal icing or sugarpaste icing covering. It is extremely pliable, and the white variety in particular takes colour well.

Marzipan can be moulded and shaped, crimped and embossed, and cut out or modelled into all kinds of animal shapes, figures, flowers, fruits, and even edible Christmas decorations, to name just a few possibilities.

Embossing

A 'pattern in relief' can be created on cakes by using special embossing tools, or any piece of kitchen equipment that will leave a patterned indentation on the marzipan. To make the embossed picture more interesting, paint on highlights with food colouring.

1 Cover the cake with marzipan, then emboss straight away before the icing dries. Dust the embossing tool with a little cornflour (cornstarch), press firmly into the marzipan, then lift off carefully to reveal the pattern. Alternatively, for a coloured design, brush a little powdered food colouring on to the embossing tool instead of the cornflour and press on to the marzipan as before.

2 ▼ Paint on coloured highlights with food colouring, if you wish.

Very simple versions of crimping and embossing have been applied to the marzipan top of this Simnel cake. The edges are crimped – or fluted – with the fingers and the top is embossed using the back of the fork.

Crimping

As with sugarpaste icing, marzipan can be crimped to give simple, pretty edgings and patterns to cakes.

1 Cover a cake with marzipan, but do not allow to dry out. To prevent the crimping tool from sticking, dip it in a little cornflour (cornstarch).

2 Place the crimping tool on the edge of the cake where it is to be decorated and then squeeze the teeth together to make the design. Slowly release the crimping tool, being careful not to let it open quickly or it will tear the marzipan.

3 ▲ Re-position the crimper and repeat to complete the design. You can decorate both the top and base edges of the cake, or the whole side of the cake, if you wish. The crimping tool can also be used to make a pattern on top of the cake.

Marzipan Cut-outs

Small flower and other shaped cutters can be purchased from cake icing specialists for cutting out marzipan shapes. Aspic, cocktail or biscuit cutters can also be used. Once you have cut out the basic shapes, you can decorate them with different coloured marzipan trims, small sweets or piping. Here are some ideas for cut-out marzipan flowers.

COLOURFUL BLOSSOMS

▲ Colour the marzipan to the desired shades. Roll out evenly on a work surface lightly dusted with icing sugar. Dip the ends of a leaf cutter or a small round cutter in icing (confectioners') sugar, and cut out five petals for each flower. Overlap the petals in a circle, securing with a little water. Shape small balls of yellow or orange marzipan and place one in the centre of each flower.

FRILLY BLOSSOMS AND LEAVES

▲ Colour and roll out the marzipan as for the Colourful Blossoms. For each flower, cut out two circles using two fluted cutters, one slightly smaller than the other. (The sizes will depend on the size of flower you are making.) To frill the edges, position the end of a wooden cocktail stick (toothpick) over 3 mm/⅛ inch of the outer edge of each circle. Roll the stick firmly back and forth around the edges with your finger so the edges become thinner and begin to frill. Continue until the circles are completely frilled.

Place the smaller frill on top of the larger, and lightly press together to secure. Take a small ball of the deeper shade of marzipan and press through a fine sieve. Cut off the marzipan which has been pushed through the strainer and place in the centre of the flower.

Cut out leaves from green marzipan with a leaf cutter. Bend the leaves slightly to make them look more life-like. Larger leaves can be left to bend over the handle of a wooden spoon until firm.

VIOLETS

▲ Colour the marzipan purple and roll out as for the Colourful Blossoms. Cut out each flower with a four-petal cocktail cutter. With a little yellow marzipan, shape small balls and then position in the centre of each flower.

Creative cut-outs – marzipan can be used in unusual ways to make imaginative shapes and borders.

Braiding and Weaving

Use these techniques with marzipan to make colourful edgings and decorations for cakes.

CANDY-STRIPE ROPE

1 Take two pieces of different coloured marzipan. On a work surface lightly dusted with icing (confectioners') sugar, roll out two or three ropes of even length and width with your fingers.

2 ▲ Pinch the ends together at the top, then twist into a rope. Pinch the other ends to seal neatly.

BRAID

1 Take three pieces of different coloured marzipan. On a work surface lightly dusted with icing sugar, roll out three ropes of even length and width with your fingers.

2 ▲ Pinch the ends together at the top, then braid the ropes neatly and pinch the other ends to seal neatly.

MARZIPAN TWIST

1 Colour the marzipan (working with one or two colours). On a work surface lightly dusted with icing (confectioners') sugar, roll out each piece of marzipan to a 5 mm/¼ inch thickness, then cut each piece into 1 cm/½ inch wide strips.

2 ▲ Take two different coloured strips and pinch the ends together at the top. Twist the strips together, joining on more strips with water, if needed.

BASKET-WEAVE

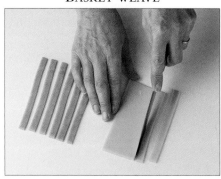

1 ▲ On a work surface lightly dusted with icing (confectioners') sugar, roll out a piece of marzipan (or work with two colours and roll out each one separately) to a 5 mm/¼ inch thickness. Cut into 5 mm/¼ inch wide strips.

2 ◄ Arrange the strips, evenly spaced, in parallel lines, then weave the strips in and out. Alternate the colours if using two, as shown. This decoration looks stunning on top of a cake. The edges can be trimmed to fit the shape of the cake.

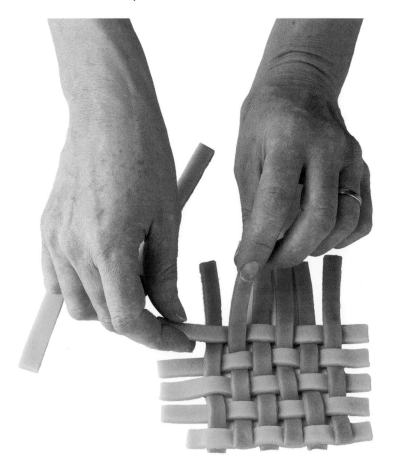

Marzipan Roses

Not only do these roses smell sweet, they taste good too. Though they may look difficult to make, marzipan roses are quite simple to mould. For a formally decorated cake, shape the roses in a variety of colours and sizes, then arrange flamboyantly on top.

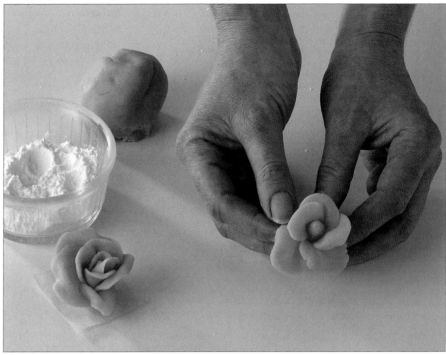

1 ▲ Take a small ball of coloured marzipan and form it into a cone shape. This forms the central core which supports the petals.

2 ▲ To make each petal, take a small piece of marzipan about the size of a large pea, and work it with your fingers to a petal shape which is slightly thicker at the base. If the marzipan sticks, dust your fingers in icing (confectioners') sugar or cornflour (cornstarch).

3 ▲ Wrap the petal around the cone as shown. Press the petal to the cone to secure. Bend the ends of the petal back slightly, to curl.

4 ▲ Mould the next petal in the same way and attach as before, so it just overlaps the first one. Curl the ends back slightly. Repeat with several more petals, making them slightly bigger until you have the size of rose you want. Overlap each petal and curl the ends back as before. Make sure all the petals are securely attached, then cut off the base of the cone. This provides a flat surface so the rose will stand on the cake.

5 For rosebuds, make just a few smaller petals and do not curl the ends back.

6 To add more detail to the rose, paint tints on to the petals using a paintbrush and food colouring. Leave to stand on baking parchment until firm.

Blooming roses – moulded roses can add glamour to any cake.

Decorating with Butter Icing

Butter icing is very quick to make up and is easy to use for quick and simple decorations. It can be used to sandwich cakes together, or to coat the top and sides with a thick, creamy layer of icing. To make your butter-iced cakes a little more individual, texture the icing on the tops or sides – or both if you wish. To finish, you can pipe the icing in swirls.

Cake Sides

For decorating cake sides, all you need is a plain or serrated scraper, depending on whether you want a smooth or a textured finish to the icing. If you have an icing turntable, it will make icing cake sides a much simpler task, but it is not essential.

Here a chocolate-flavoured and green-coloured butter icing have been realistically swirled to imitate tree bark and leaves in this delightful novelty cake idea.

1 ▲ Secure the cake to a cake board with a little icing. Cover the top and sides of the cake with icing and put it on an icing turntable. Using a plain or serrated scraper, hold it with one hand firmly against the side of the cake at a slight angle.

2 ▲ Turn the turntable round in a steady continuous motion and in one direction with the other hand, while pulling the scraper smoothly in the opposite direction to give a smooth or serrated surface to the iced sides. When you have completed the full turn, stop the turntable and carefully lift off the scraper to leave a neat join. Trim off any excess icing from the top edge and the cake board.

Cake Tops

More intricate patterns can be made on the tops of cakes with a few simple tools. Use a small palette knife, a plain or serrated scraper or a fork to give a silky smooth finish to the cake, or to make a variety of patterned ridges or some deep, generous swirls.

SWIRLS

1 ▲ Spread the icing smoothly over the top of the cake, then work over the icing with the tip of a palette knife from side to side to create a series of swirled grooves.

2 For a more formal appearance, draw the tip of a palette knife through the swirled grooves in evenly spaced lines.

RIDGED SPIRAL

1 Spread the icing smoothly over the top of the cake, then place the cake on a turntable.

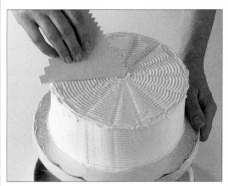

2 ▲ Hold a serrated scraper at a slight angle, pointing it towards the centre of the cake. Rotate the cake with your other hand, while moving the scraper sideways to make undulations and a ridged spiral pattern.

FEATHERED SPIRAL

1 Spread the icing smoothly over the top of the cake and place the cake on a turntable. Rotate the turntable slowly, drawing the flat tip of a palette knife in a continuous curved line, starting from the edge of the cake and working in a spiral into the centre.

2 ▲ Pull out lines with the tip of the knife, radiating out from a central point to the edge of the cake.

RIDGED SQUARES

1 Spread the icing smoothly over the top of the cake. Pull a fork across the cake four or five times, depending on the size of the cake, to produce groupings of evenly spaced lines.

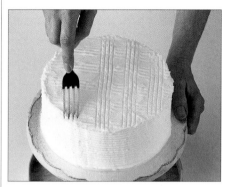

2 ▲ Pull the fork across the cake four or five times as before, but at right angles to the first lines, to give a series of large squares.

DIAMONDS

1 Spread the icing smoothly over the top of the cake. Then lightly dredge with unsweetened cocoa powder, if using white or lightly tinted butter icing, or icing (confectioners') sugar if using chocolate icing.

2 ▲ Draw a series of lines with the flat side of a knife to expose the butter icing and to make a diamond pattern over the top.

Decorating with Glacé Icing

Using white and coloured glacé icing, simple but effective patterns can be created for decorating sponges, Madeira cakes or Swiss rolls. To vary the ideas shown here using one colour of icing, make up two colours of icing and pipe them alternately. Glacé icing sets quickly but needs to be very soft to create the following designs, so make a batch just before you want to decorate the cake and work quickly before it hardens.

Cobweb, Feather and Fan Icing

Cobweb, feather and fan effects are created using the same basic technique. For the cobweb, the coloured lines are piped in circles. For the fan, the colour is applied in straight lines and the skewer is pulled across in radiating lines. For feather icing the skewer is pulled at right angles through them.

COBWEB ICING

1 Make the glacé icing, colour a portion and put in a paper piping bag, as for feather icing. Coat the top of the cake evenly with the remaining white icing.

2 ▲ Work quickly before the icing has a chance to set. Pipe evenly spaced circles on top of the icing, starting from the centre of the cake and moving towards the edge.

3 ▲ Using a skewer, pull it in straight lines from the edge of the cake to the centre so that it is evenly divided into four sections.

4 ▲ Working from the centre of the cake to the edge, pull the skewer between the four lines to divide the cake evenly into eight. Leave to set.

For an effective Spider's web cake, use the cobweb icing technique. First cover the cake with yellow glacé icing. Pipe a continuous spiral of black glacé icing, then draw a skewer down from the top at regular intervals.

FEATHER ICING

1 Make the glacé icing (see page 27, Basic Icing Recipes). Put 2 tbsp of the icing in a small bowl and colour with a little food colouring.

2 Fit a paper piping bag with a No 2 writing nozzle, then spoon in the coloured icing and fold over the top of the bag to secure.

3 ▼ Coat the top of the cake evenly with the remaining white icing. Working quickly so the icing does not set, pipe the coloured icing in straight lines across the cake. You may find it easier to work from the centre outwards when doing this.

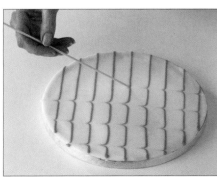

4 ▲ Using a skewer, pull it at right angles through the coloured lines in one direction, leaving an even spacing between the lines.

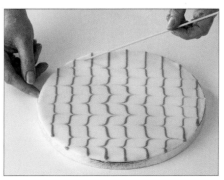

5 ▲ Working in the space between the lines, pull the skewer in the opposite direction, to give a feather pattern. Leave to set.

FAN ICING

1 Make the glacé icing, colour a portion and put in a paper piping (pastry) bag. Ice the top of the cake as for the Feather and Cobweb techniques.

2 Working quickly so the icing does not set, pipe the coloured icing in evenly spaced straight lines across the cake. You may find it easier to work from the centre outwards.

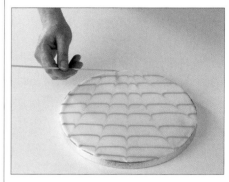

3 ▲ Using a skewer, pull it through the coloured lines, starting from a point at one edge of the cake and radiating the lines out from it.

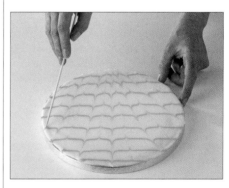

4 ▲ Working in the space between the lines, pull the skewer through the piped lines in the opposite direction to give a fan pattern. Leave to set.

ecorating with Chocolate

Nothing adds a luxurious touch to a cake quite like chocolate, whether it is poured over to form a glossy icing, or piped, shaved, dipped or curled. There are several types of chocolate to choose from, and all should be used with care. Couverture is the best and used for professional chocolate work, but it is expensive and requires particularly careful handling. For the following techniques, good-quality baking or eating chocolate is suitable. Chocolate-flavoured cake covering is easy to use but is inferior both in taste and texture.

Chocolate decorations can look particularly interesting if different kinds of chocolate – dark (bittersweet), milk and white – are used in combination. White chocolate can be coloured, but make sure you use powdered food colouring for this as liquid colourings will thicken it. Store chocolate decorations in the refrigerator in a plastic container between layers of baking parchment until ready to use. Also, handle the decorations as little as possible with your fingers, as they will leave dull marks on the shiny surface of the chocolate.

Melting

For most of the decorations described in this section, the chocolate must be melted first.

1 ▼ Break the chocolate into small pieces and place in a bowl set over a pan of hot water. Do not allow the bowl to touch the water and do not let the water boil; the chocolate will spoil if overheated. Melt the chocolate slowly and stir occasionally. Be careful not to let water or steam near the chocolate or it will become too thick.

2 ▲ When the chocolate is completely melted, remove the pan from the heat and stir.

Coating Cakes

1 ▲ Stand the cake on a wire rack. It is a good idea to place a sheet of baking parchment or a baking sheet underneath the rack to catch any chocolate drips. Pour the chocolate icing over the cake quickly, in one smooth motion, to coat the top and sides.

2 Use a palette knife to smooth the chocolate over the sides, if necessary. Allow the chocolate to set, then coat with another layer, if wished.

Piping with Chocolate

Chocolate can be piped directly on to a cake, or it can be piped on to baking parchment to make run-outs, small outlined shapes or irregular designs. After melting the chocolate, allow it to cool slightly so it just coats the back of a spoon. If it still flows freely it will be too runny to hold its shape when piped. When it is the right consistency, you then need to work fast as the chocolate will set quickly.

Chocolate Outlines

Pipe the chocolate in small, delicate shapes to use as elegant decorations on cakes. Or pipe random squiggles and loosely drizzle a contrasting chocolate over the top.

1 Melt 115 g/4 oz chocolate and allow to cool slightly. Tape a piece of baking parchment to a baking sheet or flat board.

2 ▼ Fill a paper piping (pastry) bag with the chocolate. Cut a small piece off the pointed end of the bag in a straight line. Pipe your chosen shape in a continuous line, and repeat or vary. Leave to set in a cool place, then lift off the paper with a palette knife.

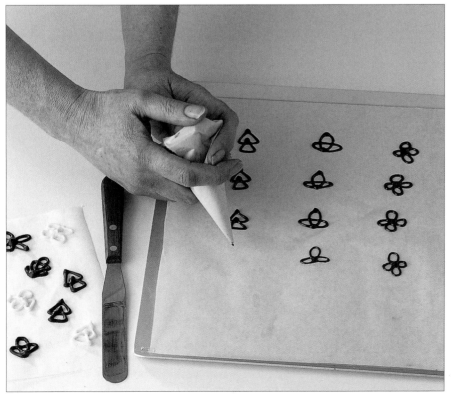

Piping on to Cakes

This looks effective on top of a cake iced with coffee glacé icing.

1 Melt 50 g/2 oz each of white and dark (bittersweet) chocolate in separate bowls and allow to cool slightly. Place the chocolates in separate paper piping (pastry) bags. Cut a small piece off the pointed end of each bag in a straight line.

2 ▲ Hold each piping bag in turn above the surface of the cake and pipe the chocolates all over. Here, the chocolates have been piped in overlapping semi-circles of different sizes. Try your own designs, too.

Chocolate Lace Curls

Make lots of these curly shapes and store them in a cool place ready for using as cake decorations. Try piping the lines in contrasting colours of chocolate to vary the effect.

1 ▲ Melt 115 g/4 oz chocolate and allow to cool slightly. Cover a rolling pin with baking parchment and attach it with tape. Fill a paper piping bag with the chocolate and cut a small piece off the pointed end in a straight line.

2 ▲ Pipe lines of chocolate backwards and forwards over the baking parchment, as shown.

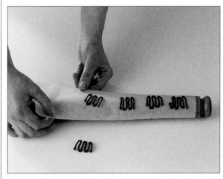

3 ▲ Leave the chocolate lace curls to set in a cool place, then carefully peel off the parchment.

Marbling Chocolate — Chocolate Run-Outs

Here, dark (bittersweet) chocolate is swirled over a white glacé-iced cake for a stunningly simple effect. Before melting the chocolate, make the icing, then work very quickly while both the chocolate and the icing are still soft.

The same basic method used for making royal icing run-outs is used here with chocolate. Try piping the outline in one colour of chocolate and filling in the middle with another.

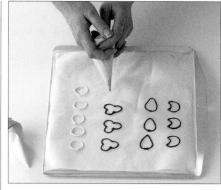

1 Melt 50 g/2 oz of dark (bittersweet) chocolate. Coat the top of the cake evenly with white glacé icing.

2 ▲ Spoon the chocolate into a paper piping bag, cut a small piece off the pointed end in a straight line and then quickly pipe the chocolate in large, loose loops.

3 ▼ Pull a cocktail stick through the chocolate in short, swirling movements and in different directions, to create a random marbled effect.

1 ▲ Tape a piece of baking parchment to a baking sheet or flat board. Draw around a shaped biscuit cutter on to the paper, or trace or draw a shape of your choice freehand. Repeat the design several times.

2 Secure a piece of baking parchment over the top of the pencilled design. Tape it down securely at the corners with masking tape.

3 ▲ Fill two paper piping (pastry) bags with melted chocolate. Cut a small piece off the pointed end of one of the bags in a straight line and pipe over the outline of your design in a continuous thread.

4 ▲ Cut the end off the other bag, slightly wider than before, and pipe the chocolate to fill in the outline so it looks slightly rounded. Leave to set in a cool place, then carefully lift off the paper with a palette knife.

Chocolate icing and decorating techniques are demonstrated in all their glory on this sumptuous chocolate gâteau. The cake is covered with fudge frosting. A neat ring of cocoa is then dusted around the edge, using a round stencil to protect the centre of the cake. The cake is decorated with mottled white and plain chocolate leaves. Chocolate curls adorn the top, and haphazardly piped white chocolate shapes, loosely overpiped with dark chocolate, complete the ultimate chocoholic extravaganza.

Chocolate Leaves

Chocolate leaves are made by coating real leaves with dark (bittersweet), white or milk chocolate or any combination of the three. Choose small freshly-picked leaves with simple shapes and well-defined veins, such as rose leaves. Leave a short stem on the leaves so you have something to hold.

1 ▲ Wash and dry the leaves well on kitchen paper. Melt 115 g/4 oz chocolate. Using a paintbrush, brush the underside of each leaf with chocolate. Take care not to go over the edge of the leaf or the chocolate will be difficult to peel off.

2 ▲ Using different chocolates for a mottled effect, brush the leaves in the same way, partly with plain (semisweet) or milk and partly with white chocolate.

3 Place the leaves chocolate-side up on baking parchment. Leave to set.

4 ▲ Carefully peel the leaf from the chocolate, handling the chocolate as little as possible. If the chocolate seems too thin, re-coat with more melted chocolate. Leave to set.

Chocolate Cut-Outs

You can make abstract shapes, or cir-cles, squares and diamonds, by cutting them out freehand with a sharp knife. Alternatively, use a large biscuit cutter or ruler as a guide, or cut out the shapes with small biscuit or cocktail cutters. These shapes look equally attractive whether evenly positioned around the sides of the cake, spaced apart or over-lapping each other, or simply arranged haphazardly.

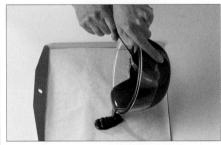

1 ▲ Cover a baking sheet with baking parchment and tape down at each corner. Melt 115 g/4 oz dark, milk or white chocolate. Pour the chocolate on to the baking parchment.

2 ▲ Spread the chocolate evenly with a palette knife. Allow to stand until the surface is firm enough to cut, but not so hard that it will break. It should no longer feel sticky when touched with your finger.

3 ▲ Press the cutter firmly through the chocolate and lift off the paper with a palette knife. Try not to touch the surface of the chocolate or you will leave marks on it.

4 ▲ The finished shapes can be left plain or piped with a contrasting chocolate if you wish.

5 ▲ Abstract shapes can be cut with a knife freehand. They look particularly effective pressed on to the sides of a butter iced cake.

Chocolate-dipped Fruit and Nuts

Use small, fresh fruit such as strawberries, grapes and kumquats for dipping, and whole nuts such as almonds, cashews, brazils or macadamias. Make sure that the fruit and nuts are at room temperature, or the chocolate will set too quickly.

1 Line a baking sheet with baking parchment. Wash the fruit and dry well on kitchen paper. Hold the fruit by its stem, then dip into the chocolate. You can either coat the piece of fruit completely, or just dip half of it, leaving the line of chocolate straight or at a slight angle. Remove the fruit, shake it gently and let any excess chocolate fall back into the bowl. Place on baking parchment and leave to set.

2 ▲ For nuts, place a nut on the end of a long kitchen fork or dipping fork. Lower into the chocolate and coat completely. Lift out of the chocolate and shake off any excess, then leave to set as for fruit. To coat just half of the nut, hold it between your fingers and dip part way into the chocolate.

3 For a two-tone effect, melt dark and white chocolate in separate bowls. Dip the fruit or nuts into one colour to coat completely, then, when set, half-dip into the other colour.

Chocolate Curls

1 Melt 115 g/4 oz chocolate. Pour the chocolate on to a firm, smooth surface such as a marble, wood or plastic laminate, set on a slightly damp cloth to prevent slipping. Spread the chocolate evenly over the surface with a large palette knife.

2 ▲ Leave the chocolate to cool slightly. It should feel just set, but not hard. Hold a large sharp knife at a 45° angle to the chocolate and push it along the chocolate in short sawing movements from right to left and left to right to make curls.

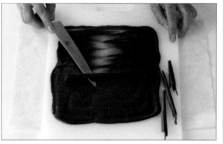

3 ▲ Remove the curls by sliding the point of the knife underneath each one and lifting off. Leave until firm.

Chocolate Shavings

The quickest way to turn chocolate into a decoration is simply to grate or shave it. The chocolate should be at room temperature for this.

1 ▲ For fine shavings, grate the chocolate on the coarse side of a grater. For coarser shavings, peel off curls with a vegetable peeler.

This sophisticated heart-shaped cake is a wonderful idea for Valentine's Day or to celebrate an engagement. It is completely covered with rich, dark chocolate curls.

Cake Recipes

The recipes you'll find here include innovative as well as classic designs for much-loved favourites to cater for every taste and any occasion. There are many special treats to try, from simple decorated sponge cakes to sumptuous gâteaux, and a heavenly chocolate-iced anniversary cake to a wonderful royal-iced wedding extravaganza.

One-stage Victoria Sandwich

Originally made in an oblong shape, today's Victoria sandwich is made using a variety of different flavourings and decorations, and is baked and cut into all sorts of shapes and sizes. Use this basic recipe to suit the occasion.

INGREDIENTS
Serves 6–8
*175 g/6 oz/1¹/₂ cups self-raising (self-rising) flour
pinch of salt
175 g/6 oz/³/₄ cup butter, softened
175 g/6 oz/³/₄ cup caster (superfine) sugar
3 eggs*

To Finish
*4–6 tbsp raspberry jam
caster (superfine) sugar or icing (confectioners') sugar*

1 Preheat the oven to 180°C/375°F/ Gas 4. Grease two deep 18 cm/7 inch round cake tins (pans), line the bases with greased baking parchment.

2 ▲ Place all the ingredients in a mixing bowl and whisk together using an electric hand whisk. Divide the mixture between the prepared tins and smooth the surfaces. Bake in the centre of the oven for 25–30 minutes, or until a skewer inserted into the centre of the cakes comes out clean. Turn out on to a wire rack, peel off the baking parchment and leave to cool.

3 ▲ Place one of the cakes on a serving plate and spread with the raspberry jam. Place the other cake on top, then dredge with caster or icing sugar, to serve.

Variation
Makes 8–10 iced fancies

1 ▲ Place the cake mixture in a greased and lined 23 × 33 cm/9 × 13 inch Swiss roll tin (jelly roll pan) and smooth the surface. Bake in the centre of the oven for 25–30 minutes, or until a skewer inserted into the centre of the cake comes out clean. Turn out on to a wire rack, peel off the baking parchment and leave to cool completely.

2 ▲ Cut the cake into individual sized shapes, such as fingers, diamonds, squares or small rounds, using a knife or biscuit cutters. Using one quantity of Butter Icing, cover with decorative piping. You can flavour or colour the butter icing by substituting orange or lemon juice for the milk and/or adding a few drops of food colouring.

3 For alternative decorations, you could try a selection of the following: glacé (candied) cherries, angelica, jellied fruits, grated chocolate, chopped or whole nuts, or choose one of your own ideas.

STORING
This cake can be kept for up to three days in an airtight container.

Tip

To make the decorative stencilled pattern with icing (confectioners') sugar shown here, cut out star shapes from paper. Lay the paper stars over the top of the cake and then dredge with icing sugar. Remove the paper shapes carefully to reveal the stencilled pattern.

Carrot and Almond Cake

Made with grated carrots and ground almonds, this unusual fat-free sponge makes a delicious afternoon treat.

INGREDIENTS
Serves 8–10
5 eggs, separated
finely grated zest of 1 lemon
300 g/10 oz/1⅓ cups caster (superfine) sugar
350 g/12 oz/5–6 carrots, peeled and finely grated
225 g/8 oz/1¼ cups ground almonds
115 g/4 oz/1 cup self-raising (self-rising) flour, sifted
sifted icing (confectioners') sugar, to decorate
marzipan carrots, to decorate (optional)

STORING
This cake can be kept for up to two days in an airtight container.

ip

To make the marzipan carrots, knead a little orange food colouring into 115 g/4 oz marzipan until evenly blended. On a work surface lightly dusted with icing (confectioners') sugar, divide the marzipan into walnut-sized pieces. Mould into carrot shapes and press horizontal lines along each carrot with a knife blade. Press a tiny stick of angelica into the end of each piece to resemble the carrot top. Decorate the cake with marzipan carrots.

1 Preheat the oven to 190°C/375°F/ Gas 5. Grease a deep 20 cm/8 inch round cake tin (pan), line the base with baking parchment and grease.

2 ▲ Place the egg yolks, lemon zest and sugar in a bowl. Beat with an electric mixer for about 5 minutes, until the mixture is thick and pale.

3 ▲ Mix in the grated carrot, ground almonds and flour and stir until evenly combined.

4 In a clean, dry bowl, whisk the egg whites until stiff. Using a large metal spoon or rubber spatula, mix a little of the whisked egg whites into the carrot mixture, then fold in the rest.

5 ▲ Spoon the mixture into the prepared cake tin and bake in the centre of the oven for about 1¼ hours, or until a skewer inserted into the centre of the cake comes out clean. Leave the cake in the tin for about 5 minutes, then turn out on to a wire rack, peel off the baking parchment and leave to cool completely.

6 ▲ Decorate with sifted icing sugar and marzipan carrots.

Jewel Cake

This pretty tea-time cake is excellent served as an afternoon treat with tea or coffee.

INGREDIENTS
Serves 10–15
115 g/4 oz/1/2 cup mixed coloured
glacé (candied) cherries, halved,
washed and dried
50 g/2 oz/1/4 cup stem ginger in
syrup, chopped, washed and dried
50 g/2 oz/1/3 cup chopped mixed
(candied) peel
115 g/4 oz/1 cup self-raising
(self-rising) flour
75 g/3 oz/3/4 cup plain
(all-purpose) flour
25 g/1 oz/3 tbsp cornflour
(cornstarch)
175 g/6 oz/3/4 cup butter
175 g/6 oz/3/4 cup caster
(superfine) sugar
3 eggs
finely grated zest of 1 orange

To Decorate
175 g/6 oz/11/2 cups icing
(confectioners') sugar, sifted
2–3 tbsp freshly squeezed
orange juice
50 g/2 oz/1/4 cup mixed coloured
glacé (candied) cherries, chopped
25 g/1 oz/21/2 tbsp mixed
(candied) peel, chopped

STORING
This cake can be kept for up to two days in an airtight container.

Tip

To ring the changes, bake the cake in a 18 cm/7 inch round cake tin (pan), if wished. Use the same quantities of ingredients and follow the method as described here. Decorate with crystallized citrus fruits instead of the glacé (candied) cherries and mixed (candied) peel.

1 Preheat the oven to 180°C/350°F/ Gas 4. Grease a 900 g/2 lb loaf tin (pan), line the base and sides with baking parchment and grease.

2 ▲ Place the cherries, stem ginger and mixed peel in a plastic bag with 25 g/1 oz/1 tbsp of the self-raising flour and shake to coat evenly. Sift the remaining flours and cornflour into a small bowl.

3 ▲ Place the butter and sugar in a mixing bowl and beat until light and fluffy. Beat in the eggs, one at a time, until evenly blended. Fold in the sifted flours with the orange zest, then stir in the dried fruit.

4 ▲ Transfer the cake mixture to the prepared tin and bake in the centre of the oven for about 11/4 hours, or until a skewer inserted into the centre of the cake comes out clean. Leave the cake in the tin for about 5 minutes, then turn out on to a wire rack, peel off the lining paper and leave to cool completely.

5 ▲ To decorate the cake, place the icing sugar in a mixing bowl. Stir in the orange juice and mix until smooth. Drizzle the icing over the cake. Mix together the chopped glacé cherries and mixed peel in a small bowl, then use to decorate the cake. Allow the icing to set before serving.

Strawberry Cream Gâteau

Fresh raspberries also work well for this recipe.

3 ▲ Bake in the centre of the oven for 30–35 minutes or until a skewer inserted into the centre of the cake comes out clean. Turn out on to a wire rack, peel off the baking parchment and leave to cool completely.

4 ▲ To make the strawberry cream, place all but one of the strawberries in a food processor or blender and purée until smooth. Place the double cream in a mixing bowl and whisk until it holds peaks. Fold the purée into the cream with the icing sugar and liqueur.

5 ▲ Place the cooled cake on a plate and spread the strawberry cream evenly over the top and sides, making swirls for an attractive finish. Decorate with the sliced reserved strawberry.

INGREDIENTS
Serves 8–10
2 egg yolks
4 eggs
finely grated zest of 1 lemon
115 g/4 oz/½ cup caster (superfine) sugar
115 g/4 oz/1 cup plain (all-purpose) flour, sifted
115 g/4 oz/½ cup butter, melted

For the Strawberry Cream
225 g/8 oz/1½ cups fresh strawberries, washed, dried and hulled
275 ml/½ pint/1¼ cups double (heavy) cream
50 g/2 oz/½ cup icing sugar
1 tbsp strawberry liqueur or Kirsch

STORING
This cake can be kept for up to two days in the refrigerator.

1 Preheat the oven to 150°C/300°F/ Gas 2. Grease a 20 cm/8 inch round cake tin (pan), line the base with baking parchment, then grease.

2 Place the eggs yolks, egg, lemon zest and sugar in a mixing bowl and beat with an electric mixer for about 10 minutes or until thick and pale. Add the flour and melted butter. Whisk for a further minute, then transfer to the prepared cake tin.

Simnel Cake

A traditional cake for Easter.

INGREDIENTS
Serves 10–12
225 g/8 oz/1 cup butter, softened
225 g/8 oz/1 cup caster (superfine)
sugar
4 eggs, beaten
550 g/1¼ lb/3 cups mixed dried fruit
115 g/4 oz/½ cup glacé
(candied) cherries
3 tbsp sherry (optional)
275 g/10 oz/2½ cups plain
(all-purpose) flour, sifted
3 tsp mixed (apple pie) spice
1 tsp baking powder
675 g/1½ lb yellow marzipan
1 egg yolk, beaten
ribbons and sugared eggs,
to decorate

STORING
This cake can be kept for up to two
weeks in an airtight container.

1 Preheat the oven to 160°C/325°F/
Gas 3. Grease a deep 20 cm/8 in
round cake tin, line with a double
thickness of baking parchment and
grease the parchment.

2 Place the butter and sugar in a large
mixing bowl and beat until light
and fluffy. Gradually beat in the eggs.
Stir in the dried fruit, glacé cherries and
sherry, if using.

3 ▲ Sift together the flour, mixed
spice and baking powder, then fold
into the cake mixture. Set aside.

4 ▲ Cut off half of the marzipan and
roll out on a work surface lightly
dusted with icing sugar to a 20 cm/
8 inch round. Spoon half of the cake
mixture into the prepared tin (pan) and
smooth the surface with the back of a
spoon. Place the marzipan round on
top, then add the other half of the cake
mixture and smooth the surface.

5 Bake in the centre of the oven for
about 2½ hours or until golden and
springy to the touch. Leave the cake in
the tin for about 15 minutes, then turn
out on to a wire rack, peel off the lining
paper and leave to cool completely.

6 ▲ Roll out the other half of the
marzipan to a round to fit on top of
the cooled cake. Brush the top of the
cake with a little of the egg yolk and
position the marzipan round on top.
Flute the edges of the marzipan and, if
liked, make a decorative pattern on top
with a fork. Brush with more egg yolk.

7 Put the cake on a baking sheet and
place under a grill for 5 minutes or
until the top is lightly browned. Leave
to cool completely before decorating
with ribbons and sugared eggs.

Black Forest Gâteau

A perfect gâteau for a special occasion tea party, or for serving as a sumptuous dessert at a dinner party.

INGREDIENTS
Serves 10–12
5 eggs
175 g/6 oz/³⁄₄ cup caster (superfine) sugar
50 g/2 oz/¹⁄₂ cup plain (all-purpose) flour, sifted
50 g/2 oz/¹⁄₃ cup unsweetened cocoa powder, sifted
75 g/3 oz/6 tbsp butter, melted

For the Filling
5–6 tbsp Kirsch
575 ml/1 pint/2¹⁄₂ cups double (heavy) cream
1 x 425 g/15 oz can black cherries, drained, stoned and chopped

To Decorate
225 g/8 oz plain chocolate
15–20 fresh cherries, preferably with stems
sifted icing sugar (optional)

STORING
This cake is not suitable for storing.

1 Preheat the oven to 180°C/350°F/ Gas 4. Grease two deep 20 cm/8 inch round cake tins (pans), line the bases with greased baking parchment.

2 ▲ Place the eggs and sugar in a large mixing bowl and beat with an electric mixer for about 10 minutes or until the mixture is thick and pale.

3 Sift together the flour and cocoa powder, then sift again into the whisked mixture. Fold in very gently, then slowly trickle in the melted butter and continue to fold in gently.

4 Divide the mixture between the tins and smooth the surfaces. Bake in the centre of the oven for about 30 minutes, or until springy to the touch. Leave in the tin for about 5 minutes, then turn out on to a wire rack, peel off the lining paper and leave to cool.

5 ▲ Cut each cake in half horizontally and lay on a work surface. Sprinkle the four layers with the Kirsch.

6 ▲ In a large bowl, whip the cream until it holds soft peaks. Transfer two-thirds of the cream to another bowl and stir in the chopped cherries. Place a layer of cake on a serving plate or cake board and spread over one-third of the filling. Top with another layer of cake and continue layering, finishing with a layer of cake.

7 Use the remaining whipped cream to cover the top and sides of the gâteau, spreading it evenly with a knife.

8 To decorate the gâteau, melt the chocolate in a bowl over a pan of hot water, or in a double boiler. Spread the chocolate out on to a plastic chopping board and allow to set.

9 ▲ Using a long sharp knife, scrape along the surface of the melted chocolate to make thin shavings and use these to cover the sides of the cake and to decorate the top. Finish by arranging the cherries on top of the gâteau. Dust with sifted icing sugar, if wished.

Tip

If liked, the cherries can be coated or half-coated in chocolate before arranging on the cake. To do this, reserve 2–3 tbsp of the melted chocolate and dip the cherries into it. Allow the dipped cherries to set on baking parchment.

Vegan Chocolate Gâteau

It isn't often that vegans can indulge in a slice of chocolate cake and this one tastes so delicious, they'll all be back for more!

INGREDIENTS
Serves 8–10

300 g/10 oz/2¹/₂ cups self-raising
(self-rising) wholemeal
(whole-wheat) flour
50 g/2 oz/¹/₃ cup unsweetened
cocoa powder
3 tsp baking powder
250 g/9 oz/1¹/₄ cups caster
(superfine) sugar
few drops of vanilla extract
9 tbsp sunflower oil
350 ml/12 fl oz/1¹/₂ cups water
sifted unsweetened cocoa powder,
to decorate
25 g/1 oz/¹/₄ cup chopped nuts,
to decorate

For the Chocolate Fudge
50 g/2 oz/¹/₄ cup vegan
(soya) margarine
3 tbsp water
250 g/9 oz/2¹/₃ cups icing
(confectioners') sugar
2 tbsp unsweetened cocoa powder
1 – 2 tbsp hot water

STORING
This cake can be kept for up to two days in the refrigerator.

1 Preheat the oven to 170°C/325°F/ Gas 3. Grease a deep 20 cm/8 inch round cake tin (pan), line the base and sides with baking parchment and grease the parchment.

2 Sift the flour, cocoa powder and baking powder into a large mixing bowl. Add the caster sugar and vanilla essence, then gradually beat in the sunflower oil and water to make a smooth batter.

3 Pour the cake mixture into the prepared tin and smooth the surface with the back of a spoon.

4 ▲ Bake in the centre of the oven for about 45 minutes or until a skewer inserted into the centre of the cake comes out clean. Leave in the tin for about 5 minutes, then turn out on to a wire rack, peel off the baking parchment and leave to cool. Cut the cake in half.

5 ▲ To make the chocolate fudge, place the margarine and water in a pan and heat gently until the margarine has melted. Remove from the heat, add the sifted icing sugar and unsweetened cocoa powder, beating until smooth and shiny. Allow to cool until firm enough to spread and pipe.

6 ▲ Place the bottom layer of cake on a serving plate and spread over two-thirds of the chocolate fudge mixture. Top with the other layer of cake. Fit a piping (pastry) bag with a star nozzle, fill with the remaining chocolate fudge and pipe stars over the cake. Sprinkle with unsweetened cocoa powder and chopped nuts.

Exotic Celebration Gâteau

Use any tropical fruits you can find to make a spectacular display of colours and tastes.

INGREDIENTS
Serves 8–10
175 g/6 oz/¾ cup butter, softened
175 g/6 oz/¾ cup caster
(superfine) sugar
3 size 3 eggs, beaten
250 g/9 oz/2¼ cups self-raising
(self-rising) flour
2–3 tbsp milk
6–8 tbsp light rum
425 ml/¾ pt/scant 2 cups
double (heavy) cream
25 g/1 oz/¼ cup icing
(confectioners') sugar, sifted

To Decorate
450 g/1 lb mixed fresh exotic and
soft fruits, such as figs, redcurrants,
kiwi fruit, etc.
6 tbsp apricot jam, warmed
and strained
2 tbsp warm water
sifted icing (confectioners') sugar

STORING
*This cake can be kept for up to two
days in the refrigerator.*

1 Preheat the oven to 190°C/375°F/
Gas 5. Grease and flour a deep
20 cm/8 inch ring mould.

2 ▲ Place the butter and sugar in a
mixing bowl and beat until light
and fluffy. Gradually beat in the eggs,
then fold in the flour with the milk.

3 Spoon the cake mixture into
the prepared tin and smooth the
surface. Bake in the centre of the oven
for about 45 minutes, or until a skewer
inserted into the centre of the cake
comes out clean. Turn out on to a wire
rack and leave to cool completely.

4 ▲ Place the cake on a serving plate,
then use a thin skewer to make
holes randomly over the cake. Drizzle
over the rum and allow to soak in.

5 ▲ Place the cream and icing sugar
in a mixing bowl and beat with an
electric mixer until the mixture holds
soft peaks. Spread all over the top and
sides of the cake.

6 Arrange the fruits attractively in the
hollow centre of the cake, allowing
the fruits to overhang the edges a little.
Mix together the apricot jam and water,
then use to brush evenly over the fruit.
Sift over a little icing sugar, to decorate.

Chocolate Chestnut Roulade

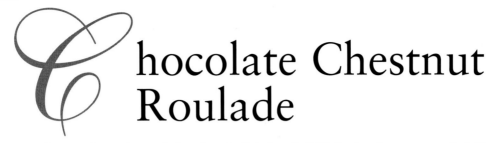

A traditional version of the classic Bûche de Nöel, the famous and delicious French Christmas gâteau.

INGREDIENTS
Serves 6–8
225 g/8 oz plain (semisweet) chocolate
50 g/2 oz white chocolate
4 eggs, separated
114 g/4 oz/¹/₂ cup caster (superfine) sugar, plus extra for dredging

For the Chestnut Filling
150 ml/¹/₄ pint/²/₃ cup double (heavy) cream
1 x 225 g/8 oz can chestnut purée
4–5 tbsp icing (confectioners') sugar, plus extra for dredging
1–2 tbsp brandy

STORING
This cake can be kept for up to two days in the refrigerator.

1 Preheat the oven to 180°C/350°F/ Gas 4. Grease a 23 × 33 cm/ 9 × 13 inch Swiss roll tin (jelly roll pan), line with greased baking parchment.

2 Place 50 g/2 oz of the plain chocolate and the white chocolate in two bowls and set over pans of hot water. Stir until melted.

3 ▲ Pour the plain chocolate on to a plastic chopping board and spread out evenly. When just set, do the same with the white chocolate. Leave to set.

4 To make the chocolate curls, hold a long, sharp knife at a 45° angle to the chocolate and push it along the chocolate, turning the knife in a circular motion. Carefully place the plain and white chocolate curls on a baking sheet lined with baking parchment and set aside until needed.

5 ▲ Place the remaining plain chocolate in another bowl set over a saucepan of hot water and stir until melted. Set aside. Place the egg yolks and caster sugar in a mixing bowl and beat with an electric mixer until thick and pale. Stir in the chocolate.

6 Whisk the egg whites in a clean dry bowl, until they hold stiff peaks. Fold into the chocolate mixture and then turn into the prepared tin. Bake in the centre of the oven for 15–20 minutes, or until risen and firm. Place on a wire rack, cover with a just-damp cloth and leave to cool completely.

7 Place a sheet of baking parchment on the work surface and sprinkle with a little caster sugar. Turn the roulade out on to the baking parchment. Peel away the parchment and trim the edges of the roulade. Cover again with a just-damp cloth.

8 To make the filling, whip the double cream in a mixing bowl, until it holds soft peaks.

9 ▲ Place the chestnut purée and icing sugar in a clean bowl. Add the brandy and beat until smooth and evenly combined, then fold in the whipped cream.

10 ▲ Spread the mixture over the roulade, leaving a little border at the top edge. Roll up the roulade, using the greaseproof paper to help and transfer it to a serving plate. Top with the chocolate curls and sprinkle with sifted icing sugar, to serve.

Daisy Christening Cake

A ring of moulded daisies sets off this pretty pink christening cake. It can be made in easy stages, giving time for the various icings to dry before adding the next layer.

INGREDIENTS
Serves 20–25
20 cm/8 inch round Rich Fruit Cake
3 tbsp apricot jam, warmed and strained
675 g/1½ lb marzipan
900 g/2 lb/1⅓ x quantity Royal Icing
115 g/4 oz/⅓ quantity Sugarpaste Icing
pink and yellow food colourings

MATERIALS AND EQUIPMENT
25 cm/10 inch round cake board
5 cm/2 inch fluted cutter
wooden cocktail stick
2 greaseproof paper piping (pastry) bags
No 42 nozzle
pink and white ribbon

STORING
The finished cake can be kept for up to three months in an airtight container.

1 Brush the cake with the apricot jam. Roll out the marzipan on a work surface lightly dusted with icing (confectioners') sugar and use to cover the cake. Leave to dry for 12 hours.

2 Secure the cake to the cake board with a little of the icing. Colour three-quarters of the icing pink. Flat ice the cake with three or four layers of smooth icing, using the white icing for the top and the pink for the sides. Allow each layer to dry overnight before applying the next. Set aside a little of both icings in airtight containers, to decorate the cake.

3 Meanwhile, make the daisies. You will need about 28. For each daisy cut off a small piece of sugarpaste icing. Dust your fingers with a little cornflour (cornstarch) to prevent sticking.

4 ▲ Shape the icing with your fingers to look like a golf tee, with a stem and a thin, flat, round top.

5 ▲ Using scissors, make small cuts all the way around the edge of the daisy. Carefully curl the cut edges slightly in different directions. Place the daisies on a sheet of baking parchment to dry.

6 ▲ When dry, trim the stems and paint the edges with pink and the centres with yellow food colouring.

7 ▲ To make the plaque, roll out the remaining sugarpaste icing on a work surface lightly dusted with icing sugar and cut out a circle with the fluted cutter. Position the end of a wooden cocktail stick over 5 mm/¼ inch of the outer edge of the circle. Roll the stick firmly back and forth around the edge with your finger until the edge becomes thinner and begins to frill. Continue until the edge of the plaque is completely frilled. Place on a sheet of baking parchment to dry, then paint the name in the centre of the plaque and the edges with pink food colouring.

8 ▲ Fit a paper piping (pastry) bag with the nozzle and pipe a twisted rope around the top and bottom edges of the cake with the remaining white royal icing. Wash the nozzle, fit it in a fresh paper piping bag and pipe a row of stars around the top of the cake with the remaining pink icing.

9 Secure the plaque to the centre of the cake with a little royal icing. Arrange the daisies on the cake, also securing with the icing, and decorate with the ribbons.

Rose Blossom Wedding Cake

The traditional white wedding cake, with its classic lines and elegant piping, is still a favourite choice for many brides and grooms.

INGREDIENTS
Serves 80
*23 cm/9 inch square Rich Fruit Cake
15 cm/6 inch square Rich Fruit Cake
75 ml/7 tbsp apricot jam, warmed
and strained
1.5 kg/3½ lb marzipan
1.5 kg/3½ lb/2⅓ x quantity Royal
Icing, to coat
675 g/1½ lb/1 quantity Royal Icing,
to pipe
pink and green food colourings*

MATERIALS AND EQUIPMENT
*28 cm/11 inch square cake board
20 cm/8 inch square cake board
No 1 writing and No 42 nozzles
several baking parchment
piping (pastry) bags
thin pink ribbon
8 pink bows
3–4 cake pillars
about 12 miniature roses
few fern sprigs*

STORING
*The finished cake can be kept
for up to three months in an
airtight container.*

1 Brush the cakes with the apricot jam and cover with marzipan, allowing 450 g/1 lb marzipan for the 15 cm/6 inch cake and the remainder for the 23 cm/9 inch cake. Place the cakes on the cake boards and leave to dry for 12 hours.

2 Make the royal icing for coating the cake. Secure the cakes to the cake boards with a little of the icing. Flat ice the cakes with three or four layers of smooth icing, allowing each layer to dry overnight before applying the next. The royal icing should be very dry before assembling the cake, so it can be made to this stage and stored in cardboard cake boxes for several days.

3 Make the royal icing for piping, and colour a small amount pale pink and another small portion pale green. To make the piped sugar pieces, draw the double-triangle design on a piece of baking parchment several times. You will need 40 pieces, but make extra in case of breakages. Tape the paper to a baking sheet or flat board and secure a piece of baking parchment over the top. Tape it down at the corners.

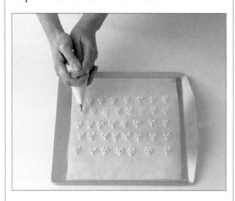

4 ▲ Fit a piping bag with a No 1 writing nozzle. Half-fill with white royal icing and fold over the top to seal. Pipe over each design, carefully following the outlines with a continuous thread of icing. Spoon a little of the pink icing and a little of the green icing into separate paper piping bags fitted with No 1 writing nozzles. Pipe pink dots on the corners of the top triangle in each design and green on the corners of the bottom triangle in each design. Leave to dry for at least two hours.

5 Mark four triangles on the top and side of each cake with a pin. Work from the centre of each side, so each triangle is 6 cm/2½ inches wide at the base and 4 cm/1½ inches high on the smaller cake, and 7.5 cm/3 inches wide at the base and 5 cm/2 inches high on the larger cake. Fit a paper piping bag with a clean No 1 writing nozzle and half-fill with some of the white icing. Using the pin marks as a guide, pipe double lines to outline the triangles.

6 ▲ Using the same nozzle, pipe cornelli inside all the triangles.

7 ▲ Fit a piping bag with a No 42 nozzle and half-fill with white icing. Pipe shells around the top and bottom edges of each cake, but not within the triangles.

8 Using the piping bags fitted with No 1 writing nozzles and filled with pink and green icing, pipe dots on the corners of each cake.

9 ▲ Remove the piped sugar pieces from the paper by carefully turning it back and lifting off each piece with a palette knife. Secure them to the cake and cake board with a little icing.

10 Decorate the cake with the ribbon and bows. Just before serving, assemble the cake with the cake pillars and decorate with the roses and fern sprigs.

Fudge-frosted Starry Roll

Whether it's a birthday or another occasion you are wanting to celebrate,
this sumptuous looking cake is sure to please.

INGREDIENTS
Serves 8
1 quantity Swiss Roll mix
½ quantity chocolate-flavour
Butter Icing
50 g/2 oz white chocolate
50 g/2 oz plain (semisweet)
chocolate
1½ x quantity Fudge Frosting

MATERIALS AND EQUIPMENT
23 x 33 cm/9 x 13 inch Swiss
roll tin (jelly roll pan)
small star cutter
several baking parchment
piping (pastry) bags
No 19 star nozzle

STORING
This cake can be kept for up to two
days in an airtight container
in the refrigerator.

1 Preheat the oven to 180°C/350°F/ Gas 4. Grease the tin (pan), line the base with baking parchment and grease. Spoon in the cake mixture and gently smooth the surface. Bake for about 12–15 minutes, or until springy to the touch.

2 Turn out on to a sheet of baking parchment lightly sprinkled with caster (superfine) sugar, peel off the lining paper and roll up the Swiss roll, leaving the parchment inside. When cold, unroll carefully, remove the paper and spread the cake with the butter icing. Re-roll and set aside on a sheet of baking parchment on a wire rack.

3 ▲ To make the chocolate decorations, cover a board with baking parchment and tape down at each corner. Melt the white chocolate, then pour on to the baking parchment. Spread the chocolate evenly with a palette knife and allow to stand until the surface is firm enough to cut, but not so hard that it will break. It should no longer feel sticky when touched with your finger. Press a small star cutter firmly through the chocolate and lift off the paper with a palette knife. Set aside.

4 ▲ Melt the plain chocolate and allow to cool slightly. Cover a rolling pin with baking parchment and attach it with tape. Fill a paper piping bag with the chocolate and cut a small piece off the pointed end in a straight line. Pipe lines of chocolate backwards and forwards over the baking parchment, to the size you choose. Make at least nine curls so you have extra in case of breakages. Leave the chocolate lace curls to set in a cool place, then carefully peel off the paper.

5 ▲ Make the fudge frosting. When cool enough to spread, cover the Swiss roll with about two-thirds of it, making swirls with a palette knife.

6 ▲ Fit a fresh paper piping bag with the No 19 star nozzle and spoon in the remaining frosting. Pipe diagonal lines, like a twisted rope, on either side of the roll and across both ends.

7 ▲ Position the lace curls in the icing, and arrange the stars. Transfer the cake to a serving plate and decorate with more stars.

Christmas Tree Cake

No piping is involved in this bright and colourful Christmas tree cake, making it a good choice for all the family to help decorate.

INGREDIENTS
Serves 20 – 25
20 cm/8 inch round Rich Fruit Cake
3 tbsp apricot jam, warmed and strained
900 g/2 lb marzipan
green, red, yellow and purple food colourings
225 g/8 oz/⅓ quantity Royal Icing
silver balls

MATERIALS AND EQUIPMENT
25 cm/10 inch round cake board

STORING
The finished cake can be kept for up to three months in an airtight container.

1 Brush the cake with the apricot jam. Colour 675 g/1½ lb of the marzipan green. Roll out the green marzipan on a work surface lightly dusted with icing (confectioners') sugar and use it to cover the cake. Leave to dry for 12 hours.

2 ▲ Make the royal icing. Secure the cake to the cake board with a little of the icing. Spread the icing evenly on the side of the cake to cover just half way up. Starting at the bottom of the cake, press the flat side of a palette knife into the icing, then pull away sharply to form a peak. Repeat until the iced area is covered with peaks.

3 ▲ Draw three Christmas tree shapes in different sizes on to a piece of card and cut out. Take half of the remaining marzipan and colour it a slightly deeper shade of green than the top. Using the card templates as a guide, cut out three Christmas tree shapes. Arrange the trees on top of the cake.

4 ▲ Divide the remaining marzipan into three portions and colour it red, yellow and purple. Use a little of the marzipan to make five 9 cm/3 inch rolls from each colour. Loop the coloured lengths alternately around the top edge of the cake, pressing on to the top to secure firmly.

5 ▲ Make small balls from red marzipan and press on to the end of each loop.

6 ▲ Use the remaining marzipan to make the tree decorations. Roll the red marzipan into a thin rope and cut into eight 2.5 cm/1 inch lengths for the candles. Shape eight flames from the yellow icing and stick on the end of each candle. Mould 11 small balls from the purple icing and press a silver ball into the centre of each.

7 Arrange the candles and balls on the trees, securing them with a little water if necessary.

Hallowe'en Pumpkin Patch

Pumpkins have sprung up all over this orange and chocolate cake, making it the ideal design to celebrate Hallowe'en.

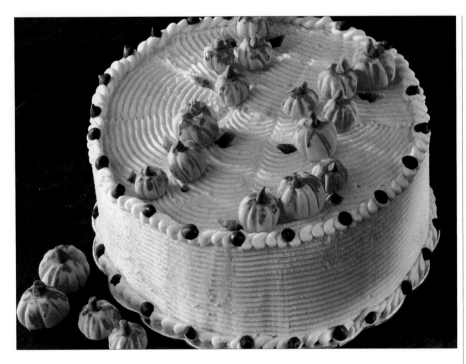

INGREDIENTS
Serves 12–15
*2 x quantity chocolate-flavour
Quick-Mix Sponge Cake mix
175 g/6 oz/2 x quantity
Sugarpaste Icing
orange and brown food colourings
2 x quantity orange-flavour
Butter Icing
chocolate chips
angelica*

MATERIALS AND EQUIPMENT
*2 x 20 cm/8 inch round cake
tins (pans)
23 cm/9 inch round cake board
serrated scraper
greaseproof paper piping
(pastry) bag
No 7 writing nozzle*

STORING
*This cake can be kept for up to
three days in the refrigerator.*

1 Preheat the oven to 160°C/325°F/ Gas 3. Grease the cake tins, line the bases with baking parchment and grease the parchment.

2 Divide the mixture between the tins and smooth the surfaces. Bake for 20–30 minutes or until firm to the touch. Turn out on to a wire rack, peel off the parchment and leave to cool.

3 ▲ To make the pumpkins, colour a very small piece of the sugarpaste icing brown, and the rest orange. Dust your fingers with a little cornflour (cornstarch). Shape small balls of the orange icing the size of walnuts and some a bit smaller. Make the ridges with a wooden cocktail stick. Make the stems from the brown icing and press into the top of each pumpkin, securing with water. Paint highlights on each pumpkin with orange food colouring. Leave to dry on baking parchment.

4 Cut each cake in half horizontally. Use one-quarter of the butter icing to sandwich the cakes together. Place the cake on the cake board. Use about two-thirds of the remaining icing to coat the top and sides of the cake.

5 Texture the cake sides with a serrated scraper. Decorate the top with the same scraper, moving the scraper sideways to make undulations and a ridged spiral pattern in a slight fan shape. The texturing should resemble a ploughed field.

6 ▲ Fit a paper piping bag with the writing nozzle and spoon in the remaining butter icing. Pipe a twisted rope pattern around the top and bottom edges of the cake.

7 Decorate the piping with chocolate chips.

8 ▲ Cut the angelica into diamond shapes and arrange on the cake with the pumpkins.

Easter Egg Nest Cake

Celebrate Easter with a fresh-tasting lemon sponge, colourfully adorned with marzipan nests and chocolate eggs.

INGREDIENTS
Serves 10
1 quantity lemon-flavour Quick-Mix Sponge Cake mix
350 g/12 oz/1 quantity lemon-flavour Butter Icing
225 g/8 oz marzipan
pink, green and purple food colourings
foil-wrapped chocolate eggs

MATERIALS AND EQUIPMENT
20 cm/8 inch ring mould
25 cm/10 inch cake board

STORING
This cake can be kept for up to three days in an airtight container in the refrigerator.

1 Preheat the oven to 160°C/325°F/ Gas 3. Grease and flour the ring mould. Spoon the cake mixture into the mould and smooth the surface. Bake in the centre of the oven for about 25 minutes, or until firm to the touch. Turn out on to a wire rack and leave to cool completely.

2 ▲ Cut the cake in half horizontally and sandwich together with about one-third of the butter icing. Position the cake on the cake board. Spread the remaining icing over the outside of the cake to cover completely.

3 Smooth the top of the cake with a palette knife and swirl the icing around the side of the cake.

4 ▲ To make the marzipan plaits, divide the marzipan into three portions and colour it pink, green and purple. Cut each portion in half. Using one-half of each of the colours, roll each one out with your fingers on a work surface lightly dusted with icing (confectioners') sugar to make a thin sausage shape long enough to go around the bottom edge of the cake. Pinch the ends together at the top, then twist the individual strands into a rope. Pinch the other ends to seal neatly.

5 ▲ Place the rope on the cake board around the bottom edge of the cake.

6 To make the nests, take the remaining portions of coloured marzipan and divide each colour into five. Roll each piece into a rope about 16 cm/6½ inches long. Take a rope of each colour, pinch the ends together, twist to form a multi-coloured rope and pinch the other ends. Form the rope into a circle and repeat to make the remaining four nests.

7 ▲ Arrange the nests so they are evenly spaced on the top of the cake and place several chocolate eggs in the middle of each.

Cloth of Roses Cake

This cake says 'congratulations' for whatever reason – passing an exam, getting a new job, getting engaged, or for just achieving a lifelong ambition.

INGREDIENTS
Serves 20–25
*20 cm/8 inch round Light
Fruit Cake
3 tbsp apricot jam, warmed
and strained
675 g/1½ lb marzipan
900 g/2 lb/2⅔ x quantity
Sugarpaste Icing
yellow, orange and green
food colourings
115 g/4oz/¹⁄₆ quantity Royal Icing*

MATERIALS AND EQUIPMENT
*25 cm/10 inch cake board
7 cm/2¾ inch plain cutter
petal cutter
thin yellow ribbon*

STORING
*The finished cake can be stored
for up to four weeks in an
airtight container.*

1 Brush the cake with apricot jam. Roll out the marzipan on a work surface lightly dusted with icing (confectioners') sugar and cover the cake. Leave for 12 hours.

2 Cut off 675 g/1½ lb of the sugarpaste icing and divide in half. Colour one-half very pale yellow and the other very pale orange. Wrap separately in clear film (plastic wrap) and set aside.

3 Cut out a template for the orange icing from baking parchment, as follows. Draw a 25 cm/10 inch circle using the cake board as a guide. Using the plain cutter, draw half circles 2.5 cm/1 inch wide all around the outside of the large circle. Cut out the template.

4 Roll out the yellow sugarpaste icing on a work surface lightly dusted with icing sugar to the same length and height as the side of the cake. Brush the side of the cake with a little water and cover with the sugarpaste icing. Position the cake on the cake board.

5 ▲ Roll out the orange sugarpaste icing to about a 30 cm/12 inch circle. Place the template on the icing and cut out the scalloped shape.

6 ▲ Brush the top of the cake with water and cover with the orange icing so the scallops fall just over the edge. Bend them slightly to look like a cloth. Leave to dry overnight.

7 Meanwhile make the roses and leaves. Cut off about three-quarters of the remaining sugarpaste icing and divide into four portions. (Wrap the other piece in clear film and reserve for the leaves.) Colour the four portions pale yellow, deep yellow, orange, and marbled yellow and orange.

8 ▲ For each rose, dust your fingers with cornflour (cornstarch), take a small ball of coloured icing and form into a cone shape. For each petal, take a small piece of icing and work it with your fingers into a petal shape which is slightly thicker at the base. Wrap the petal around the cone so it sits above the top of it, pressing together to stick. Curl the ends of the petal back. Mould the next petal and attach so it just overlaps the first one. Curl the ends back. Repeat with several more petals, making them slightly larger each time. Cut off the base so the rose will stand on the cake. Make about 18 roses. Leave to dry on baking parchment.

9 ▲ Colour the reserved piece of sugarpaste icing green for the leaves. Roll out thinly and cut out leaves with a petal cutter. Make about 24 leaves. Leave to dry on baking parchment.

10 Arrange the leaves and roses, securing with a little royal icing. Decorate the cake with the ribbon.

Birthday Parcel

*Here is a birthday cake that is all wrapped up and ready to eat.
The pattern on the iced present can be changed by
using different shaped cutters.*

3 ▲ Roll out the orange and green icings and use the same cutters to cut out circles and triangles. Replace the exposed holes in the blue icing with the orange and green shapes, easing in to fit. Gather together the orange and green trimmings.

4 ▲ Roll out the orange trimmings and cut three strips about 2 cm/ ³/₄ inch wide and long enough to go over each corner of the cake. Roll out the green trimmings and cut three very thin strips the same length as the orange ones. Place the orange and green strips next to each other to give three striped ribbons, and secure the pieces together with a little water.

5 Place one striped ribbon over one corner of the cake, securing with a little water. Place a second strip over the opposite corner.

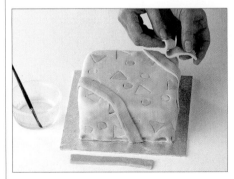

6 ▲ Cut the remaining ribbon in half. Bend each half to make loops and attach both to one corner of the cake with water to form a loose bow.

INGREDIENTS
Serves 10
15 cm/6 in square Madeira Cake
³/₄ quantity orange-flavour
Butter Icing
3 tbsp apricot jam, warmed
and strained
450 g/1 lb/1¹/₃ x quantity
Sugarpaste Icing
blue, orange and green food colourings

MATERIALS AND EQUIPMENT
15–18 cm/7–8 inch square cake board
small round and triangular
cocktail cutters

STORING
*The finished cake can be kept for up
to one week in an airtight container.*

1 Cut the cake in half horizontally and sandwich together with the butter icing. Brush the cake with apricot jam. Colour three-quarters of the sugarpaste icing blue. Divide the remaining sugarpaste icing in half and colour one-half orange and the other half green. Wrap the orange and green sugarpaste separately in plastic wrap and set aside. Roll out the blue icing on a work surface lightly dusted with icing (confectioners') sugar and use it to cover the cake. Position on the cake board.

2 While the sugarpaste covering is still soft, cut out circles and triangles from the blue icing with the cocktail cutters, lifting out the shapes to expose the cake beneath.

Chocolate-iced Anniversary Cake

This cake is special enough to celebrate any wedding anniversary. Tropical fruits and a glossy chocolate icing make it very appealing for all ages.

INGREDIENTS
Serves 12–15
20 cm/8 inch round Madeira Cake
1½ x quantity chocolate-flavour
Butter Icing
1 quantity Satin Chocolate Icing
chocolate buttons
selection of fresh fruits, such as
kiwi, nectarine or peach, apricot,
physalis

MATERIALS AND EQUIPMENT
baking parchment piping
(pastry) bag
No 22 star nozzle
thin gold ribbon, about 5 mm/
¼ in wide
florist's wire

STORING
This cake can be kept for up to five
days in the refrigerator.

1 Cut the cake into three horizontal layers and sandwich together with about three-quarters of the chocolate butter icing. Place the cake on a wire rack with a baking sheet underneath.

2 ▲ Make the satin chocolate icing and immediately pour over the cake to coat completely. Working quickly, ease the icing gently over the surface of the cake, using a palette knife if necessary. Allow to set.

3 ▲ Transfer the cake to a serving plate. Fit a paper piping bag with the star nozzle and spoon in the remaining chocolate butter icing. Pipe scrolls around the top edge of the cake.

4 Cut several chocolate buttons into quarters and use to decorate the butter icing.

5 ▲ Prepare the fruit for the top of the cake. Peel and slice the kiwi and cut into quarters, and slice the nectarine or peach, apricot and physalis.

6 Arrange the fruit on top of the cake. For each ribbon decoration, make two small loops using the thin gold ribbon. Twist a piece of florist's wire around the ends of the ribbon to secure the loops. Trim the ends of the ribbon. Cut the wire to the length you want and use it to put the loops in position on the cake. Make about seven ribbon decorations. Remove the ribbons and wire before serving.

Golden Wedding Heart Cake

Creamy gold colours, delicate frills and dainty iced blossoms give this cake a special celebratory appeal.

INGREDIENTS
Serves 30
23 cm/9 inch round Rich Fruit Cake
4 tbsp apricot jam, warmed
and strained
900 g/2 lb marzipan
900 g/2 lb/2⅔ x quantity
Sugarpaste Icing
cream food colouring
115 g/4 oz/⅙ quantity Royal Icing

MATERIALS AND EQUIPMENT
28 cm/11 inch round cake board
crimping tool
small heart-shaped plunger tool
7.5 cm/3 inch plain cutter
dual large and small blossom
cutter stamens
frill cutter
foil-wrapped chocolate hearts

STORING
The finished cake can be kept
for up to three months in an
airtight container.

1 Brush the cake with apricot jam. Roll out the marzipan on a work surface lightly dusted with icing (confectioners') sugar and use it to cover the cake. Leave to dry for 12 hours.

2 Colour 675 g/1½ lb of the sugarpaste icing very pale cream. Roll out the icing on a work surface lightly dusted with icing sugar. Brush the marzipan with a little water and cover the cake with the sugarpaste icing. Position the cake on the cake board. Using a crimping tool dipped in cornflour, carefully crimp the top edge of the cake.

3 ▲ Divide the circumference of the top of the cake into eight equal sections, and stick pins in as markers. Use these as a guide to crimp evenly spaced slanting lines going from the top to the bottom edges of the cake. Using the plunger tool, emboss the bottom edge of the cake. Place the plain cutter lightly in the centre of the cake and use as a guide to emboss more hearts in a circle around the cutter. Leave the cake to dry for several hours.

4 ▲ Take the remaining sugarpaste icing and colour one-half cream and the other half pale cream. Retain half of each colour, and wrap the remainder in clear film (plastic wrap). Roll out each colour evenly and thinly. Dip the end of the blossom cutter in cornflour and cut out the flower shapes. Make a pin hole in the centre of each larger flower as you make it. Leave to dry on a foam pad. When dry, pipe a little royal icing on to a stamen and thread it through the hole of each larger flower. This will hold it in position. Allow to dry.

5 ▲ To make the frills, roll out the two shades of reserved sugarpaste icing thinly. Using the frill cutter, cut out two rings from each colour.

6 ▲ Position the end of a wooden cocktail stick over 5 mm/¼ inch of the outer edge of the ring. Roll the stick firmly back and forth around the edge with your finger until the edge becomes thinner and begins to frill. Continue until the ring is completely frilled. Repeat with remaining rings. Using a sharp knife, cut each ring in half to make two frills. You should have four frills in each shade.

7 ▲ Using a little water, attach the frills in alternate shades next to the crimped lines running down the side of the cake. Crimp the edges of the deeper coloured frills.

8 Arrange the blossom flowers on the top and side of the cake, securing with a little royal icing. Before serving, place the chocolate hearts in the centre of the cake.

Ducks on a Pond

A real treat at a children's party. A scrumptious combination of coconut cake, jelly and cream.

INGREDIENTS
Serves 8–10
1 quantity Quick-Mix Sponge
Cake mix
575 ml/1 pint/2½ cups double
(heavy) cream
green, yellow and red food
colourings
225 g/8 oz/4 cups desiccated
(dry unsweetened) coconut
1 x 135 g/4½ oz packet of green
jelly (flavoured gelatine), made up
to the manufacturer's instructions
200 g/7 oz/½ quantity
Sugarpaste Icing
a few tiny sweets
75 g/3 oz marzipan
5 pink marshmallows

MATERIALS AND EQUIPMENT
18 cm/7 inch flan tin (pan)
23 cm/9 inch round cake board
duck-shaped cutter
cocktail sticks
garlic press

STORING
The finished cake can be kept in the refrigerator for up to three days.

1 Preheat the oven to 180°C/350°F/ Gas 4. Grease the flan tin, line the base with baking parchment and grease the parchment. Spoon the cake mixture into the prepared tin and smooth the surface. Bake in the centre of the oven for 35–40 minutes or until firm to the touch. Leave the cake in the tin for about 3 minutes, then turn out on to a wire rack, peel off the lining paper and leave to cool completely.

2 ▲ Add a few drops of green food colouring to the double cream, and beat until it holds soft peaks. Place the cake on the cake board and spread the cream evenly over the cake.

3 ▲ To make the grassy bank, place the coconut in a bowl and add a few drops of green food colouring diluted with a dash of water. Stir until the coconut is speckled green and white.

4 ▲ Cut up the set jelly into 1 cm/ ½ inch pieces. Carefully place the jelly pieces in the centre of the cake.

5 To make the ducks, take 75 g/3 oz of the sugarpaste icing and colour it yellow. Roll out on a work surface lightly dusted with icing (confectioner's) sugar until about 5 mm/¼ inch thick.

6 ▲ Using a duck-shaped cutter, stamp out the ducks, then skewer the bottom of each one with a cocktail stick. Lay the ducks on a baking sheet and leave them in a warm, dry place to harden.

7 Use the tiny sweets, or sugarpaste icing, for the ducks' eyes, securing with a drop of water. Take off a small piece of marzipan, about the size of a hazelnut, then colour the remainder green and shape into a frog, using a small, sharp knife to open the mouth and make the feet. Colour the reserved piece of marzipan red, shape into the frog's tongue and secure in position with a little water. Use sweets or blue and white sugarpaste icing for the eyes. Place the frog on the cake board.

8 To make the grass, colour the remaining sugarpaste icing green and push through a garlic press, cutting it off with a small, sharp knife. Place the grass around the pond. To make the flowers, flatten the marshmallows with a rolling pin, then snip the edges with scissors to make the petals. Place the flowers around the pond and put a coloured sweet in the centre of each. The wooden cocktail sticks must be removed from the ducks before serving.

Dumper Truck

Any large, round biscuits will work well for the wheels, and all sorts of coloured sweets can go in the truck.

INGREDIENTS
Serves 8–10
1½ x quantity Quick-Mix Sponge
Cake mix
6 tbsp apricot jam, warmed
and strained
900 g/2 lb/2⅔ x quantity
Sugarpaste Icing
yellow, red and blue food colouring
icing (confectioners') sugar,
to dredge
sandwich wafer biscuits (cookies)
4 coconut swirl biscuits (cookies)
115 g/4 oz coloured sweets
5 cm/2 inch piece blue
liquorice stick
demerara (raw) sugar, for the sand

MATERIALS AND EQUIPMENT
900 g/2 lb loaf tin (pan)
30 x 18 cm/12 x 7 inch cake board
18 x 7.5 cm/7 x 3 inch piece of cake
card, brushed with apricot jam
small crescent-shaped cutter

STORING
The cake can be completed up to three days in advance and kept in a cool, dry place.

1 Preheat the oven to 180°C/350°F/ Gas 4. Grease the tin, line the base and sides with baking parchment and grease the parchment. Spoon the cake mixture into the tin and smooth the surface. Bake in the centre of the oven for 40–45 minutes or until a skewer inserted into the centre of the cake comes out clean. Turn out on to a wire rack, peel off the baking parchment and leave to cool completely.

2 Using a large, sharp knife, cut off the top of the cake to make a flat surface. Then cut off one-third of the cake to make the cabin of the truck.

3 ▲ Take the larger piece of cake, and, with the cut side up, cut a hollow in the centre, leaving a 1 cm/ ½ inch border. Brush the hollowed cake evenly with apricot jam.

4 ▲ Colour 350 g/12 oz of the sugarpaste icing yellow and remove a piece about the size of a walnut. Set aside, wrapped in clear film. Roll out the remainder on a work surface lightly dusted with icing sugar until about 5mm/¼ inch thick. Use to cover the hollowed out piece of cake, carefully pressing it into the hollow. Trim the bottom edges and set aside.

5 Colour 350 g/12 oz of the sugarpaste icing red. Cut off one-third of this and set aside, wrapped in clear film (plastic wrap). Roll out the rest on a work surface until about 5mm/¼ inch thick. Cover the remaining piece of cake and trim the edges.

6 Take the reserved red icing, break off a piece the size of a walnut and wrap in clear film. Roll out the rest and use to cover the cake card.

7 ▲ Brush the wafers with a little apricot jam and stick them together in two equal piles. Place the piles on the cake board, about 7.5 cm/3 inches apart. Place the red-covered cake card on top of the wafers. Place a little of the remaining white sugarpaste icing about halfway along the covered card in order to tip the dumper part of the truck slightly. Place the dumper on top, with the cabin in front. Stand the coconut biscuits in position for the wheels.

8 ▲ Roll out the reserved piece of yellow sugarpaste icing to make a 5 x 2.5 cm/2 x 1 inch rectangle. Colour the remaining white sugarpaste icing with blue food colouring and roll out thinly. Use the crescent-shaped cutter to stamp out the eyes. Make simple ones, or overlay with white crescent shapes for detail.

9 Roll out the reserved red sugarpaste icing thinly and stamp out a mouth shape with an appropriate cutter. Use a little water to stick the yellow panel on to the front of the truck, then stick on the features in the same way.

10 To finish, fill the dumper part of the truck with brightly coloured sweets and push a piece of coloured liquorice into the top of the cabin. Scatter the sugar around the base of the dumper truck to resemble sand.

Valentine's Box of Chocolates

This special cake would also make a wonderful gift for Mother's Day. Choose your favourite chocolates to go inside.

INGREDIENTS
Serves 10–12
1½ x quantity chocolate-flavour
Quick-Mix Sponge Cake mix
275 g/10 oz yellow marzipan
8 tbsp apricot jam, warmed
and strained
900 g/2 lb/2⅔ x quantity
Sugarpaste Icing
red food colouring
225 g/8 oz/about 16–20 hand-
made chocolates

MATERIALS AND EQUIPMENT
heart-shaped cake tin (pan)
23 cm/9 inch square piece of
stiff card
23 cm/9 inch square cake board
piece of string
small heart-shaped cutter
length of ribbon and a pin
petits fours cases

STORING
The finished cake can be kept in a cool, dry place for up to three days.

1 Preheat the oven to 180°C/350°F/ Gas 4. Grease the tin (pan), line the base with baking parchment and grease the parchment. Spoon the cake mixture into the tin and smooth the surface. Bake in the centre of the oven for 45–50 minutes, or until a skewer inserted into the centre of the cake comes out clean. Leave the cake in the tin for about 5 minutes, then turn out on to a wire rack, peel off the lining paper and leave to cool completely.

2 ▲ Place the cake on the piece of card and draw around it with a sharp pencil. Cut the heart shape out of the card and set aside. This will be used as the support for the box lid.

3 ▲ Using a large, sharp knife, cut through the cake horizontally just below where the cake starts to dome. Carefully lift the top section on to the heart-shaped card and place the bottom section on the cake board.

4 Use the piece of string to measure around the outside of the bottom section of cake.

5 ▲ On a work surface lightly dusted with icing sugar, roll out the marzipan into a long sausage shape to the same length as the string. Place the marzipan sausage on the cake around the outside edge. Brush both sections of the cake evenly with apricot jam.

6 Colour the sugarpaste icing red and cut off about one-third. Cut another portion from the larger piece, about 50 g/2 oz in weight. Wrap these two separately in clear film (plastic wrap) and set aside. On a work surface lightly dusted with icing sugar, roll out the icing to a 35 cm/14 inch square and use it to cover the bottom section of cake.

7 ▲ Stand the lid on a raised surface, such as a glass or bowl. Roll out the reserved one-third of sugarpaste icing to a 30 cm/12 inch square and cover the lid section of the cake. Roll out the remaining piece of icing and stamp out small hearts with the cutter. Stick them around the edge of the lid with a little water. Tie the ribbon in a bow and secure on top of the lid with the pin. Carefully lift the top section on to the heart-shaped card and place the bottom section on the cake board.

8 Place the chocolates in the *petits fours* cases and arrange in the bottom section of the cake. Position the lid, placing it slightly off centre, to reveal the chocolates inside. Remove the ribbon and pin before serving.

Index